Attentive To God

Thinking Theologically In Ministry

Charles M. Wood

Ellen Blue

Abingdon Press
Nashville

ATTENTIVE TO GOD
THINKING THEOLOGICALLY IN MINISTRYY

Copyright © 2008 by Abingdon Press

All rights reserved.

No part of this work may be reproduced or transmitted in any form or by any means, electronic or mechanical, including photocopying and recording, or by any information storage or retrieval system, except as may be expressly permitted by the 1976 Copyright Act or in writing from the publisher. Requests for permission should be addressed to Abingdon Press, P.O. Box 801, 201 Eighth Avenue South, Nashville, TN 37202-0801 or permissions@abingdonpress.com.

This book is printed on acid-free paper.

Library of Congress Cataloging-in-Publication Data

Wood, Charles Monroe.
  Attentive to God : thinking theologically in ministry / Charles M. Wood and Ellen Blue.
    p. cm.
  Includes bibliographical references.
  ISBN 978-0-687-65162-7 (pbk. : alk. paper)
  1. Pastoral theology.   2. Church work.   I. Blue, Ellen.   II. Title.
  BV4011.3.W66 2008
  269'.2—dc22

                                                                    2007031366

All scripture quotations unless noted otherwise are taken from the New Revised Standard Version of the Bible, copyright 1989, Division of Christian Education of the National Council of the Churches of Christ in the United States of America. Used by permission. All rights reserved.

08 09 10 11 12 13 14 15 16 17—10 9 8 7 6 5 4 3 2 1

MANUFACTURED IN THE UNITED STATES OF AMERICA

Contents

Contents

Preface

This book presents a distinctive approach to theological reflection in and on situations of pastoral leadership and, using a carefully developed array of case studies, helps its readers develop that approach and thus strengthen their own preparation for ministry. Central to the approach is the conviction that pastoral character and pastoral practice are mutually formative. The *doing* of ministry is profoundly affected by the *being* of the minister, that is, by her or his human, Christian, and pastoral identity. Conversely, it is in and through the practice of ministry that the minister's identity is both continually discovered and continually worked on and worked out. Authentic and effective pastoral leadership in any situation requires an aptitude for reading the situation—including one's own part in it—theologically. What such a theological reading of situations involves, why it is crucial to ministerial identity and practice, and how the capacity for it may be acquired and strengthened—these are the main insights to be gained through the use of this book.

The book has an introduction and three parts. The introduction sets the stage, arguing for the crucial role of theological reflection in ministry. Part 1, Becoming Theological, offers a brief orientation to Christian theology and particularly to the practice of theological reflection on situations. Part 2, Incidents and Situations, presents nineteen cases in ministry. Several of these cases share characters, settings, or themes, while others are quite independent. Part 3, Notes on Selected Cases, contains brief background interpretations or suggestions for approach for four of the cases, intended to highlight some resources and considerations that may be more broadly applicable to the theological reading of human interactions. Separating these notes from the cases themselves makes it easy for the reader to decide when, or whether, to consult them.

This book has been a collaborative effort, though with a fairly clear division of labor. Ellen Blue has written the introduction; Charles Wood, part 1. The case narratives in part 2 are Ellen Blue's work. Part 3 is the product of joint authorship. We have shared ideas throughout, and have reviewed and critiqued each other's drafts at various stages.

It should be noted that the cases are works of fiction, and not portrayals of actual incidents and situations. This is a point we have had to reiterate in our discussions of the cases with classes and groups. Students have frequently asked Charles Wood, "Where is Trinity Church?" or "Where did this happen?" Ellen Blue has never used any of the cases in any class where at least three or four individuals did not inquire, "How did you know about my church?"

I want to record my gratitude to a number of companions on the journey toward this book. By their thoughtful participation in case study in various modes, students in several classes and workshops at Perkins School of Theology over the past several years have enhanced my understanding of the process and have demonstrated its fruitfulness. Those discussions have also helped us improve the presentation of some of the cases included in this volume and refine our approach. Members of the faculty of the intern program at Perkins—Professors William J. Bryan III, Isabel Docampo, Tom Spann, Bert Affleck, and the late Virgil P. Howard—have given generously of their time and encouragement. They have graciously included me in their own examination of case study methodology and in their work with mentor pastors; have field-tested some of the cases in this book; and have regularly challenged and enriched my thinking on this subject and on theological education generally.

Charles M. Wood

Students in United Methodist doctrine classes at Phillips Theological Seminary have written and spoken insightfully about a number of the cases collected here, and have furthered this project as they did so. I thank them for their help. To another Phillips student, Matthew Thompson, I owe the suggestion that led to the case entitled "DNR." Thanks also to Susan Ruth Gray, who invited me to preach for her ordination service at First United Presbyterian Church, Fayetteville, Arkansas, on 4 December 2005. It was an occasion that led to fruitful reflection connected with this volume, and some paragraphs included in the introduction were developed for that sermon.

Ellen Blue

Introduction

S omeone once remarked that education is the only thing that people pay for and then try to get as little of as possible. Theological education may represent an extreme in this regard, since many students are admonished by the people of their churches that they should try to get absolutely nothing at all in return for the time, effort, and funds they invest in seminary training. Even students who do wish to make the most of their educations, because they recognize that the task of Christian ministry is so immense that even the most gifted need help in preparing for it, sometimes have difficulty understanding how to apply their seminary studies to their ministerial duties.

We know that in New Testament texts, the honorific "teacher" (or "rabbi") was often applied to Jesus, whose example Christians say we aspire to follow. It seems self-evident that in order to be a teacher, one must first have learned something oneself. The one small glimpse the authors of the Gospels provide about Jesus' life between toddlerhood and age thirty depicts him in the temple listening to the teachers and asking questions of them (Luke 2:41-52).

The learning that a rabbi of the first or the twenty-first century should have achieved concerns how God's people are to live together in community and in God's world. The spiritual leader is not just to know what the Scriptures say about this topic, but should also know other stories rabbis have recorded through the millennia in order to help the people, and one another, interpret those Scriptures.

The way that faithful people are to live together depends a great deal on the nature of the God whom the people worship and who calls them into community in the first place. Therefore, the Christian pastor, like the rabbi, is expected to have spent a great deal of time thinking and learning about the things of God. By the time a pastor reaches the pulpit, she or he should already have pondered deeply on questions such as: Who is God, anyway? What is God like? What is God's nature? How should we best be about worshipping our Creator? What is it that this Being wants for, and expects of, us? How is the Deity involved in the things that are happening in our world today? Does God act in our lives? And, if so, *how* does God act? How exactly are the answers we develop to these questions supposed to relate to the lives we live together as humans? And most important of all, do the answers have any bearing at all on what color we should paint the fellowship hall?

Life together as followers of Jesus is so complex. Questions about how Christian practice and Christian doctrine both spring from and determine one another are vital ones. They affect everything from life and death decisions about the beginning and ending of life to the comparatively trivial—yet often much more controversial—issues about what kind of music should be sung on Sunday morning and what kind of carpet to install in the narthex. Along the spectrum in between lie issues about how the church should attempt to meet the material needs of the poor and exactly how the sacraments should be administered.

This book concerns itself primarily with how the minister *as theologian* should see, understand, and address the practical pieces of Christian living—Christian praxis, if you will. As United Methodists, the authors have a special interest in the theological heritage of the Methodist movement's founder, John Wesley, who has often been deemed a "practical theologian." The subtext that has underlain this assessment is the idea that a practical theologian is somehow inferior to a systematic one.

In his volume on Wesleyan theology, *Responsible Grace*, Randy Maddox notes that the respected scholar Albert Outler described John Wesley's theological output as "folk theology," at first in a relatively apologetic way. Over time, Maddox asserts, Outler began to have much more respect for John Wesley as a theologian, not because he changed his mind about what Wesley was doing, but rather because he came to attach a different value to what it was that Wesley had done.

> In 1961, moving very much against the stream, [Outler] began to argue that Wesley should be valued as a major theologian. To make this case, he found it necessary to distinguish between academic theology (with its normative standard of a Systematic Theology) and Wesley's "folk theology," arguing that Wesley's value as a major theologian lay in his ability to simplify, synthesize, and communicate the essential teach-

ings of the Christian gospel to laity, not in his contributions to specula-
tive academic theology.[1]

Maddox notes that Wesley's "product," while bearing little resemblance to a textbook in systematic theology, is nevertheless full of theological material. That theology finds its expression not just in Wesley's
sermons, but also in "letters, controversial essays and tracts, conferences,
disciplinary guides for Christian life, spiritual biographies and autobiog-
raphy and a range of editorial work on creeds, liturgies, prayerbooks, Bible
study aids, hymnals, catechisms, and devotional guides."[2] Maddox used
those sources as he constructed his volume.

However, taking this recognition a step further, we might say that the
theological product of a typical parish pastor would also include nonwrit-
ten items such as administrative board or trustee meetings, fund-raising
campaigns, oversight of employees, counseling sessions, and many, many
conversations with parishioners in venues from hospital visits, to potluck
dinners, to chance encounters at the grocery store. These are the ordinary
pieces of ministry, and because we often oppose ordinary over against
sacred, it may be tempting to conclude that some ordinary duties are not
theological tasks.

On a trip to Cuba in 1997, I met a young seminary student who
expressed his desire and intention to develop a "*teología cotidiana*," an
"everyday theology." His awareness of the need for a theology that accom-
panies the practitioner in a 24/7 kind of way was astute. However, I
believed that his need to create a whole new theology for everyday use
would be obviated as he figured out how to practice the theology he was
already studying. I suspect that as he progressed in his studies, he began
to see fewer distinctions between "practical" and "systematic" theologies
and to have correspondingly less tendency to regard them as "practical"
and "impractical."

A colleague of mine uses a cyber image, unzipping files, to talk about
this process of adapting theological knowledge into the life of Christian
ministry. Files with large blocks of data may be "zipped together" for their
journey through cyberspace. The recipients cannot access and use the
data until they run a program to unzip the files, thereby making it possible to open and access the material in each one. Theological education
can sometimes resemble this process, he says, in that "you can't always use
it the way it comes."[3]

More precisely, not all students are able to decipher for themselves how the material from their systematic theology courses could or should fit into their daily work in the parish. The missing piece in many students' educations is that ability—and it is a *learned* ability—to see everyday moments as occasions to exercise skill as a trained theologian. Failure to develop this insight is what leads to a failure to connect theological learning to the everyday worklife of the Christian minister. Cultivating such insight, on the other hand, leads to a successful integration of more of what a pastor knows into more of what a pastor does.

I say "insight" because as Charles Wood writes in part 1 of this volume, the capacity of which I am speaking is, almost literally, a way of seeing—a kind of vision—that is required in order to bring all the resources acquired in theological education to bear on pastoral tasks. We might consider one of those chance encounters at the grocery store as an example.

If you are employed as a sales manager and run into your hairdresser Sunday night in the snack food section and respond to his "How are you doing?" with "I'm really frustrated. I need to finish my quarterly report, but I can't get my laptop to boot," you expect commiseration, but not much more. If you, the sales manager, run into your company's information technology specialist in aisle 3 and say, "I'm really frustrated. I need to finish my quarterly report, but I can't get my laptop to boot," you expect a different response.

The IT specialist is expected to respond differently in large part because you would expect him to have heard what you said differently—not only with expertise that allows him to understand what you are saying, and perhaps even some prior knowledge of your particular laptop, but also with a sense of responsibility for diagnosing the difficulty and getting it solved. Even a standard answer—give the computer two aspirins and call me in the morning—might still foster hope that the specialist will be standing by in the morning, marshalling resources to attack the problem.

Now suppose the encounter in aisle 3 is between you, as a pastor, and a parishioner who responds to "How are you?" with news of a parent whose physical condition is rapidly worsening and who has announced that afternoon that she is planning to discontinue dialysis. The parishioner will indeed expect an expression of sympathy, but shouldn't it differ from the expression of sympathy that a hairdresser might offer about a computer problem?

To begin with, your expression might be more artfully worded, because you may have had more experience dealing with grieving families. You might accompany your remarks with an offer of concrete assistance, such as meals delivered by the congregation's care team, since the church should be better organized to serve the bereaved than a hair salon usually is. You might hear and respond to having been alerted that a funeral or memorial service will be occurring relatively soon, since it will be your professional responsibility to see to that task, even as the IT specialist, and not the hairdresser, should expect to be seeing your computer in the immediate future.

Yet there is another distinct and important layer that a pastor should bring to the conversation. It is a theological layer that acknowledges the unspoken questions about whether discontinuing medical treatment is sinful, and how the child of the person who does so should therefore be expected to respond. It is the task of the pastor to see, acknowledge, and begin to address those questions (if only by making an appointment for a future talk), even if the parishioner is not completely aware of them yet or able to articulate them clearly. Responsibility for giving parishioners good opportunities to raise such questions and any needed assistance in phrasing them, along with offering coherent answers, belongs to those who are theologically trained.

In real life, many ministry moments have multiple layers that are by no means so easily peeled apart for examination as the supermarket encounter. The "Incidents and Situations" in part 2 of this book are intended to provide students with nineteen opportunities to practice theological thinking that have some things in common with the ways such opportunities occur in the everyday life of a minister; that is, they are enveloped inside situations that present many competing ideas and questions at the same instant. While no fictional scenario can hope to capture the layers of complexity that a real, interconnected congregation presents, there is enough texture in these cases to allow the reader to practice seeing, thinking, and reacting as a theologian. This necessitates recognizing and naming the various layers of inquiry that will appear to the pastor who has eyes to see and ears to hear.

In part 3, there are notes pointing out some of those layers for some of the cases in part 2. Looking for the theological issues yourself before turning to part 3 is an important part of the practice and can hone your theological insight. Practicing on fictional cases offers several benefits, but surely the primary benefit is that the cases are deliberately structured to give the reader time to reflect before "action" is required.

Out of my own pastoral experience, I can recall when a parishioner who sat in an ICU waiting room, hoping to hear that his thirty-something wife, who had had a dreadful stroke-like incident, would live, looked at me and asked, "Why do some people get a miracle and others don't?" I remember a twenty-eight-year-old man, who would die within the hour from a wasting disease associated with AIDS, looking up from his deathbed and asking me, "Will I be with God?" I think of a school-teacher who sat in my office and told me that she was frequently mis-placing things in her home and that her mother said demons were responsible. She laughed uncomfortably and then inquired, "Could she be right?" None of these occasions offered an opportunity to think through and choose my stance on a complicated or difficult theological issue. Real life moves at a pace markedly different from the one at which words for a book or scholarly article are chosen or at which students must read in order to grasp the nuances of a densely packed theological text.

It is at the moment when what we learn from a text is applied to a par-ticular Christian context—a particular situation in a particular time and place—that theology becomes practical theology. Immediately, though, we must recognize this assertion as a great over-simplification of the intri-cate, back-and-forth relationship that exists between Christian doctrine and Christian praxis. At least since the mid-twentieth century, the disci-pline of theology has been forced to examine its place in the development of the Christian faith, with the resultant understanding on the part of many scholars that theological reflection is a second-order activity con-ducted with and on the raw material provided by the first-order activity of Christian practice, which may or may not have been reflected upon and understood before it was performed. Ideally, then, the seminary does not seek to teach students theology so that they can go out and practice it, but rather seeks to enable students to reflect upon the Christian prac-tice in which they are already engaged, and to engage in better Christian practice and in Christian ministry that is more appropriate to their con-texts in the future.

What the case studies included in this book can offer toward the stu-dent's improved grasp of these ideas is an unusually complex and multi-layered fictional context in which to practice. The questions discussed in part 1 and at the beginning of part 2 suggest at least three areas of inquiry that should be brought to each case. There are questions about "what is going on here" from both typical and specifically theological standpoints, questions about what result you would desire to see or at least what next step should occur, and questions about what is going on for the reader and how God might be dealing with the reader as he or she works through the case.

While many readers will be tempted to move directly to the middle category, attempting to determine what should *happen* next, or what the pastor should *do*, it is important not to view the first category as a mere prelude to the "real work" of dealing with the case. "What is going on?" may prove to be the most important inquiry of all, since it is precisely the skill of seeing the situations as a trained theologian would see them that students can cultivate by using the cases.

If we changed our metaphor from vision to hearing, we could say that the work that a student accomplishes in seminary is acquiring another language, or perhaps even more aptly, learning a kind of linguistic shorthand. This does not simply mean learning what certain previously unfamiliar words mean or symbolize, though that sort of vocabulary building is vital for seminary students. The shorthand I speak of allows those who are fluent in it to say something like, "When a parishioner talks about or asks me certain things, I am able to determine quickly that although he lacks the formal language to make an efficient inquiry, what he is really asking about is, in fact, theodicy (the problem of the origin of evil)." Furthermore, even though the word *theodicy* itself may never be spoken aloud in the conversation, the theologically aware pastor has studied theodicy and reflected seriously about it and therefore has something thoughtful and helpful to say to the parishioner who is groping with a theodicy-related problem. In other words, recognizing the theological question that a parishioner who lacks a theological vocabulary is trying to articulate, and then being able to answer that question with respect to the parishioner's specific context, are among the skills that all graduates should carry with them from seminary. The first category of questions is essential to this ability.

Neither should the third category—what is going on with *you*—be simply a postlude that is attended to if there's time at the end of the work. A profound intimacy exists, or at least should exist, between the student's self-identity and his or her acts of ministry. The relationship among the Christian's being, knowing, and doing that Charles Wood discusses in "Becoming Theological," part 1 of this book, can and should be a lifelong topic of study and reflection. It is the integration of their academic work into their own past experiences and into their present and future lives in ministry that is, in my view, the single most crucial step in the successful transformation of new students into competent pastors.

John Wesley maintained that the measure of our attempt to live as Christians can be taken only by the success of our attempts to live together in Christian community, and to live *as* Christians toward the rest of society around us. It is in those areas where the trained theologian—the person "set apart" from all the other "called out" people of the church—can be at his or her very best. It is the trained theologian's particular task to remind the church of its inheritance (the good news) and of its tasks (proclaiming and implementing that gospel), to remind the church of the needs of the world, and to remind the world of what the church has to offer.

Amid all the complexities of life together, a congregation needs someone to think about the things of God all the time—much more frequently than most people have the opportunity to do—and to think about them buttressed by a sound theological education. Congregations need a good theologian to help the people reflect upon how their actions as a church affect the world God created and all of the creatures (including ourselves) whom God loves; to enable the people to live the lives to which the gospel calls them; and to empower the people to be in ministry themselves, expressing the good news creatively to the community around them. It is our hope that this book will help equip those preparing for or already serving in positions of ministerial leadership to be those good theologians.

PART ONE

BECOMING THEOLOGICAL

I .

An Understanding of Theology

One of the best brief definitions of theology I know of is one I learned from a group of experienced pastors and leaders from various church traditions some time ago: theology is a way of paying attention.[4] It is a way of paying attention to God, and to everything else in its "God-relatedness."

In thinking of theology this way, these working theologians—members of a national consultation on theological education—were indicating that for them theology was not, in the first place, the content of theological textbooks and treatises, nor the doctrines and traditions of their respective denominations. To be sure, textbooks and treatises, doctrines and traditions were not irrelevant for them, and they were not at all dismissive of their importance; but in their judgment the importance of such writings and the principles they embody has to do primarily with their role in cultivating and forming a capacity for attention.

In fact, through their experience in Christian life and ministry, these practitioners seemed to have come to have at least an implicit grasp of an old distinction among three important senses of theology. There is, first, theology as an activity: attending to reality in a certain way, struggling to understand, studying, analyzing, deliberating, forming judgments, and so forth. Second, there is theology as the product or result of that activity: the judgments or conclusions reached and then expressed in one form or another, in words or in actions—in systematic accounts of the Christian faith, in doctrinal proposals, conciliar pronouncements, sermons, hymns, liturgies, emergency relief efforts, campaigns for social justice, and so forth. (It may seem strange to think of some of these

3

things as theology; but in this second sense—theology as what emerges from theological reflection as an audible, visible, or enacted expression of an understanding of God and God's relation to things—a protest march, no less than a theological monograph, might well qualify for the term.) And finally, there is theology as an aptitude (*or habitus*) for engagement in theological reflection: a capacity and disposition to pay attention theologically. To have this aptitude in strength, we might say, is to have good theological judgment, a kind of practical wisdom. In this threefold understanding, none of the three aspects or modes of theology are to be slighted, as they are all three intimately related and interdependent. Theological writings and doctrinal formulations, for instance, are themselves among the results of attentiveness to God and to the God-relatedness of things, and if all goes well they serve to inform and strengthen our theological aptitude (to make us more attentive) and to guide our theological activity.

Among the advantages of this brief definition of theology—that it is a way of paying attention to God, and to everything else in its God-relatedness—is that it gives a certain visibility to the aptitude or *habitus* theology requires. One does not pay attention simply by deciding to. There is a discipline involved. One must become an attentive person. Theological education, in its various modalities and locations—local congregations, theological schools, internships and residency programs, and so forth—rightly centers on the development of this aptitude.

Let us try to understand a little more fully what this discipline of theology involves. We might begin by considering the *scope* of the attentiveness that we are exploring. "Scope," the dictionary tells us, can mean both "range" or "extent" (To what do we attend?) and "aim" or "purpose" (What is the point?). A similar duality of sense might be noted if we were to rephrase the question as, "What is the *object* of our attention?" Both senses are relevant here.

Our brief definition indicates that the scope of theological attention in the first sense is "God, and everything else in its God-relatedness." Implicit in this phrasing is a Christian understanding of a fundamental distinction in reality between God and "everything else": a distinction in which the "everything else" of which the world consists is apprehended as God's own beloved creation. Nothing is outside the scope of theological reflection, because there is nothing to which God is not related—as Creator first of all, but in consequence of that overarching relationship in a number of other ways as well.[5] The content and character of that rela-

4

tionship is the theme of the biblical story, and the substance of the Christian witness.

It will be useful for our purpose here to introduce a further distinction of a different sort, having to do with the "everything else" side of this fundamental distinction. H. Richard Niebuhr frames this second distinction aptly when he writes: "What is known and knowable in theology is God in relation to self and to neighbor, and self and neighbor in relation to God." He goes on:

> The nature of theology is most pertinently expressed by the Thomist and Calvinist insistence: "True and substantial wisdom principally consists of two parts, the knowledge of God and the knowledge of ourselves. But while these two branches of knowledge are so intimately connected, which of them precedes and produces the other, is not easy to discover." To the present writer it seems better to say that true and substantial wisdom consists of three parts: the knowledge of God, of companions, and of the self; and that these three are so intimately related that they cannot be separated. For self-knowledge and knowledge of the other, even though the other be the human neighbor, remain two different things.[6]

The point of this distinction between "self" and "companion" or "neighbor," if I read Niebuhr correctly, is not to introduce any sort of binary opposition between "self" and "other." Indeed, his use of "companion" and "neighbor" might be taken as a deliberate rejection of such an understanding. It is, rather, to acknowledge an important but complex fact: that the reality to which God is related, and to which we are to attend, includes ourselves, but is not limited to ourselves. Here, the "ourselves/not ourselves" distinction has several important uses. Properly appreciated, it prevents us from distancing ourselves from the scope of theological inquiry, and makes it clear that theology is a profoundly existential pursuit. It also reminds us that created reality includes more than *us*—us Christians, us human beings, or whatever other more restricted category we might find tempting—but also, as Niebuhr's wording makes clear, that the "other" in this context is co-creature, companion, neighbor. Connected with this point is still another insight: that the triadic relationship, God/self/co-creature, is (among other things that may be said of it) a moral relationship.

This brings us to the question of the scope of our theological attention, in the second sense of scope: What is the purpose or point of attending to God and to the God-relatedness of things? What end is to be served by this?

If the question itself makes us pause, it may be because it has a lot in common with "Why breathe?" or "Why fall in love?" It drives us back to basic questions about what human life is like, and what we are meant for. What (to borrow the language of the Westminster Shorter Catechism) is *our* "chief end"? We may as well see where this question leads us.

The response in the Catechism is that our chief end is "to glorify God, and to enjoy Him for ever." In many currents of Christian tradition, the human mandate to glorify God has been articulated into a threefold calling, in keeping with the notion that we are created in the image of the triune God. The language used for this varies, depending on circumstances, but there is a remarkable consistency in the substance of what is expressed. Our human vocation is to know, love, and rejoice in God, and to know, love, and rejoice in all creation in its relation to God.[7]

We human beings have a vocation to *knowledge*. The quest to know and understand, in all its varieties—exploration, discovery, research, contemplation, seeking, listening—is something we are meant for. We also have a vocation actively to *love*: to love God and neighbor, to will and work for the well-being of all. Knowledge serves love and vice versa. Finally, we have a vocation to *joy*, similarly intertwined with both knowledge and active love. Joy is not just an incidental byproduct—a guilty (or innocent) pleasure or reward accompanying some of life's events. It is a constituent aspect of our proper human responsiveness to God and to all that God has made. We are made for happiness, as Jonathan Edwards would say, as well as for knowledge and love.

I have been speaking here of our calling and purpose simply as human creatures. If paying attention to God and to all things in their God-relatedness is (as it would appear) a key and indispensable ingredient in the fulfillment of this human vocation, then all human beings are meant to be theologians—that is, meant to cultivate and exercise this kind of attentiveness in the midst of everything that they do, and everything that befalls them.

This is, of course, a Christian account of things. It is the *Christian* vocation to give such an account, and to give it in such a way that it becomes good news—good news for all, and particularly for those most afflicted by the results of humankind's ongoing defection from its true calling.

Because many of us (perhaps especially in American mainline Protestantism) are still accustomed to thinking of "Christian vocation" as

synonymous with a calling to ordained ministry, it may be well to empha-
size that in the sense in which the term is being employed here it refers
to the common calling of all Christians, a calling to the "general ministry" of the whole church. The church, as a "community of witness," a
"sign-community," a "kind of sacrament,"[8] is entrusted with a word that
it understands to be from God, about God and God's relation to all
things. That word centers in a story about Jesus of Nazareth, in whom
God's covenant with all creation was definitively and visibly enacted in
a way that has particular and decisive import for human beings. Through
the events of that story, we discover what we are meant for, and a healing is set in motion that begins to bring us into that genuine, human life.

The church bears that story into the world in a variety of ways. The
triad of Word, Sacrament, and Order commonly used in describing the
character of the church's ministry suggests a way of understanding
the variety involved, and may also hint at some connections between the
Christian vocation to bear witness to Jesus Christ, and the human vocation to which he restores us. In the way that it engages publicly in the
quest to know, to love, and to rejoice in God and God's creatures, the
church aims to help the world learn to pay attention to God.

Just as the Christian church is entrusted with this witness-bearing task,
so some members of the church are entrusted with particular responsibility (and also with particular gifts) to nurture the community as a community of witness: to "equip the saints for the work of ministry"
(Ephesians 4:12). All Christians need an aptitude for theology for the
exercise of their vocation. Pastors and other leaders in the community,
whether in congregations or in other places of responsibility, need an
abundant measure of that aptitude in order to care for the community and
see to the integrity of its witness, and to attend to their own well-being
and integrity in the process. Perhaps it was their appreciation of this
necessity that moved the men and women in ministerial leadership who
gave me this brief definition to the understanding of theology that it
expresses so well.

The Shaping of Attentiveness

Attentiveness is sometimes more, sometimes less thoughtful and self-aware. Much of the time, for those who are practiced at it, it becomes second nature, requiring no particular effort or intentionality. A theological understanding of things is almost a matter of perception, rather than of conscious investigation and interpretation. There are, however, two situations in which our attentiveness is itself likely to require a higher degree of attention: when we are learning to pay attention in the first place, or working on improving our attentiveness; and when we are facing a problem or situation that for some reason requires more deliberate scrutiny.

What informs our attentiveness? What shapes our capacity for attending to God, and guides us when we are in particular need of guidance? In keeping with Christian conviction, we should say at the outset that it is ultimately God who does so—that our learning and practice of theology, along with everything else that is good in our lives, has to do with our participation by grace in the life of the triune God, and with our being brought to understand things in the light of Jesus Christ by the Holy Spirit who is at work in us and all creation. When we speak of more proximate resources, these themselves must finally be understood in their God-relatedness, as means by which God is at work on and in and through us. (We must also keep in mind, of course, our own tendency to sabotage this work. More on this sobering fact below.)

One very helpful brief account of these resources is provided in a statement on "Our Theological Task" included in recent editions of the *Book of Discipline* of The United Methodist Church. Although it is neither exhaustive nor definitive—in this context these limitations are probably a virtue, rather than a failing—the statement identifies and discusses in an illuminating way four factors whose relevance to Christian theological reflection is widely recognized in the history of Christian thought: scripture, tradition, reason, and experience. I will draw on this account in the next few paragraphs, in the hope that the results will be useful not only to Methodists but also to readers from other branches of the Christian tradition where these factors are also very much in play.

Though United Methodists have become accustomed to referring to scripture, tradition, reason, and experience as "the Wesleyan quadrilateral," it might be better if they were to think of this group as a Wesleyan quartet. ("Wesleyan" might be traded in for some less proprietary modifier later on, but let's take one thing at a time.)[9] The analogy with an instrumental quartet in music may be helpful. Just as different instruments are not all played in the same way and do not make identical contributions to the realization of whatever music is being performed, so the different members of this quartet are brought to bear on theological reflection in different ways, for different specific purposes, though with a common end in view.

The aim is identified at the beginning of the United Methodist statement in a way that relates particularly to the church and its ministry. "As United Methodists, we have an obligation to bear a faithful Christian witness to Jesus Christ, the living reality at the center of the Church's life and witness. To fulfill this obligation, we reflect critically on our biblical and theological inheritance, striving to express faithfully the witness we make in our own time."[10] It is in order to "bear a faithful Christian witness" that we summon and employ these resources in our thinking.

What specific purposes might they serve in this enterprise of critical and constructive reflection upon the church's witness? Here, it may be worthwhile to consider three conditions that the effort to bear Christian witness, by its very nature, is obliged to satisfy, and then see how the four members of the Wesleyan quartet might come into play in addressing these requirements.

The first condition is one we may call *authenticity*. One way to understand what is at issue here is to take "heresy" as a contrast term. Authentic Christian witness is (by definition) not heretical: that is, it is not something other than Christian witness masquerading as Christian witness. Everything that the church is, says, and does as the church is under a mandate to represent Jesus Christ faithfully. "Heresy" is false witness, testimony that misrepresents Jesus Christ. Christian witness is authentic to the extent that it is actually Jesus Christ who is the content of its testimony. "How can we know the way?" Thomas asked Jesus in the upper room discourses in the Fourth Gospel, and Jesus responded, "I am the way" (John 14:5-6). The theological question we must pursue in this respect, as Karl Barth rightly framed it, is: Does the church's talk about God derive from Jesus Christ?[11]

The second condition is one we may call *truth*. In bearing, or attempting to bear, faithful Christian witness, Christians are not merely messengers, indifferent to the content of the message they are conveying. They are committed to it, as it is committed to them. They are, to put it mildly, vouching for it, underwriting it, endorsing it as "sure and worthy of full acceptance" (1 Timothy 1:15). They are bearing *testimony*. And they are bearing testimony not simply to an assortment of facts, but to the one whose identity as the truth has claimed them. They have found the Christ-event to be revelatory, that is, as H. Richard Niebuhr puts it, they have found it to be "this intelligible event which makes all other events intelligible."[12] "I am the truth," the Johannine Jesus says; and the same gospel identifies him as the *Logos*, the deep reason at the heart of things. Christians have been found by this truth, and are called to be its ministers. A popular contemporary hymn has Jesus saying to his followers, "You are the word that I intend to spread" ("*sois palabra que intento esparcir*").[13] Built into the act and substance of Christian witness is therefore a responsibility and a commitment to truth and to truthfulness. As Karl Barth puts it, the theological question that corresponds to this feature of Christian witness is: Is it in accord with Jesus Christ? Do our words, and our very existence, resonate with him, and bring the sense-making power of the Christ-event to bear upon the perplexities of human life?

The third condition we may call *fittingness*. "Fittingness" is an ungainly word, but the concept of the fitting is just what we need here. We say that an action is fitting if it meets the requirements of its circumstances—if it is the right action in the situation. It is "meet," or appropriate. The cab-driver who told the ethicist that there are times when you just have to forget your principles and do the right thing was implicitly invoking a concept of the fitting.[14] Applied to Christian witness, the condition of "fittingness" means that witness-bearing needs to be attuned to its context. Christian witness is intended to accomplish something, and it may easily fail to accomplish its purpose—indeed, it may result in something quite contrary to its purpose—if those who are bearing witness do not pay

11

attention to the context, and fit their actions to that context. The Johannine Jesus says, "I am the life." Insofar as Christian witness really becomes the Word of God proclaimed, it becomes a life-giving word. The inescapable theological question about the church's witness at this point, as Karl Barth succinctly phrased it, is: Does it lead to Jesus Christ?

Do our attempts to bear faithful Christian witness derive from Jesus Christ, who is the Way? Are they in accord with him, who is the Truth? Do they lead to him, who is the Life? Or in more prosaic terms: Is our witness authentically Christian witness? Is it true, and truthful? Is it a fitting enactment of the Word in the present context?

Elements of Theological Judgment

N ow, how might the members of the "Wesleyan quartet" be brought to bear upon our pursuit of these questions as to the authenticity, truthfulness, and fittingness of Christian witness?

None of these three conditions of faithful witness is independent of the others. Though they are distinct, the relations among them are profound and complex, and so are the relations among the three main strands of theological inquiry that correspond to them. These constitute finally one coherent inquiry. Because of this interdependence, all four members of the quartet have a role to play in addressing each of its elements. Those roles, however, are distinctive. In the sketch of the workings of theological judgment found in the United Methodist statement on these matters, tradition, experience, and reason each come to have a particular relevance to one element of the inquiry, while within each element scripture has its own unique and decisive contribution as the primary source and guideline for theological reflection. Tradition, with scripture, has a particular prominence in the quest for authenticity; reason, in the quest for truth and truthfulness; experience, with respect to the fittingness and fruitfulness of Christian witness. Each of these terms—tradition, scripture, experience, reason—names a complex reality whose adequate treatment would take us far beyond the limits of this introduction.

Various Christian denominations and confessional families will describe these factors and their interaction in different ways. However, two points of fairly broad agreement are especially pertinent to our aims in this book. The first is a widespread consensus across denominations and traditions that, just as Christian ministry and ministerial leadership involve "knowing," "being," and "doing," in intimate relation with each other, so theological education for ministry involves an education in all three of these, likewise interwoven. Some traditions speak of spiritual and personal formation ("being"), intellectual formation ("knowing"), and pastoral formation ("doing") as the three interdependent components of formation for ministry; others use different terms and conceptual schemes to describe a similar basic structure. In some traditions, a correlation between these three components of ministerial preparation and the three foci of ministry—Sacrament, Word, and Order—or the three aspects of the ministerial office—priest, teacher, and pastor—can readily be drawn. In a classical Protestant context, Martin Luther's threefold scheme for theological study—*oratio, meditatio,* and *tentatio,* or prayer, meditation, and testing—might provide the central organizing insight.[15]

The second, related point of broad agreement relevant to our purposes here is this: in describing how a theological aptitude is gained, recent writers in most Christian communities stress the central importance of a sustained and serious immersion in Christian scripture, to the point where one not only "understands scripture" (to the extent that one can be said to do so) but also "understands *through* scripture." The Brazilian theologian Clodovis Boff, reflecting the renewed emphasis on biblical study fostered by the Second Vatican Council, spoke of the "hermeneutical competency" or "hermeneutical *habitus*" that is developed through the discipline of reading the Bible in community: an ability to read the present situation and one's present experience "according to the scriptures."[16] The interplay of the members of the "Wesleyan quartet" is again brought out in this observation, as is the primary role of Scripture in fostering theological attentiveness.

Vision and Discernment

The noted philosopher and historian of ideas Sir Isaiah Berlin (1909–1997) began an essay on Leo Tolstoy by quoting an obscure line from the Greek poet Archilochus and then giving it a figurative interpretation. The line, as Berlin rendered it in English, was, "The fox knows many things, but the hedgehog knows one big thing." Berlin acknowledges that the words "may mean no more than that the fox, for all his cunning, is defeated by the hedgehog's one defence." But he sets out to take them figuratively, to represent "one of the deepest differences which divide writers and thinkers, and, it may be, human beings in general." The difference is between, on the one hand, those "who relate everything to a single central vision, one system, less or more coherent or articulate, in terms of which they understand, think, and feel," and, on the other hand, "those who pursue many ends, often unrelated and even contradictory, connected, if at all, only in some *de facto* way."[17] Thinkers of the first type Berlin calls hedgehogs; those of the second, foxes. The hedgehog sees the big picture or the universal principle, and is keen to interpret everything in terms of that. The fox sees details, and is fascinated by them.

After giving some examples of famous hedgehogs and foxes (as he would classify them) in the history of European thought, Berlin quickly acknowledges that the distinction is not so hard and fast, and that many thinkers—including Leo Tolstoy, the subject of the essay in which he ventures this comparison—embody a mixture of both tendencies, though it is often an uneasy mixture and not a harmonious blend.

Assuming that most human beings exercise both of these ways of thinking, though no doubt in differing proportions and in a variety of relations to each other, the applicability of this distinction to our subject deserves some thought. Theological attentiveness, it would seem, requires a constant movement between just these two modalities: between attentiveness as *vision* (the hedgehog's gift) and attentiveness as *discernment* (the fox's specialty).[18] Paying attention theologically involves "seeing things whole": making connections, understanding how things hang together, seeking coherence—the work of synthesis. This is vision. It also involves seeing particular things in their particularity, and not letting them be "interpreted away"; understanding, and respecting, differences; caring for details—the work of analysis. This is discernment. These two modalities of perception and judgment are not independent of each other. They require each other. The tension between them is a creative tension. It may also generate a certain amount of discomfort, especially if Berlin is right in thinking that people tend to gravitate toward one or the other of these poles, and to find the other a distraction or an inconvenience.

In cultivating theological attentiveness, both modalities must be nurtured in close interaction with each other. Achieving the appropriate balance and relationship may be difficult, not only on account of our temperamental differences in this regard but also in part because of the different contexts and approaches required for cultivating the aptitude for vision and the aptitude for discernment. At the level of graduate theological education, for example, vision is typically more readily fostered in the context of coursework than is discernment. Textbooks and monographs and lectures tend to summarize and synthesize knowledge, organizing data into interpretative schemes, offering principles and categories to aid learners in making sense of things. To be sure, there are exceptions: books can be written and courses can be designed and taught in such a way as to develop discernment. But it is in the nature of both books and courses to bring ideas (and people) together, and to aim at offering or constructing interpretations rather than at the mere confrontation of learners with data. Discernment, on the other hand, may be more readily fostered in the context of practical experience, living through actual situations in the setting of an internship, practicum, or residency, in "lived time" rather than in the condensed and compressed reality of books and classrooms.

This contrast, like Berlin's original division between hedgehogs and foxes, may be overdrawn. In contemporary theological education there

16

are deliberate efforts underway to overcome the compartmentalization of these modalities of learning into separate domains, in the growing recognition that neither vision nor discernment will thrive in the absence of the other. To cultivate vision—which is not a prefabricated picture imposed upon reality but rather a capacity and disposition to see one thing in relation to other things, to see or seek out connections, and to understand how individual things in mutual interaction constitute some larger intelligible whole—is at the same time to sharpen discernment, in that differences can only be perceived and appreciated in some context. Likewise, to cultivate discernment is at the same time to improve vision. The theologian Douglas John Hall writes of the dangers inherent in the enterprise of "systematic" theology: "The very adjectives *systematic* and *dogmatic* (or even the less blatant *constructive*) betray a predilection to permanency. It so easily happens that a (right and good) desire to 'see things whole,' to integrate, to describe connections, to honor the unity of truth and so on becomes, in its execution, an exercise in finality."[19] Before we fit new data neatly into their preassigned places in the account we have constructed, it is vital to pause long enough to ask ourselves in what ways these new data challenge our account and call for some re-visioning. In this way vision is enriched by discernment, just as discernment is enhanced by vision.

The aptly named twentieth-century British philosopher John Wisdom writes in one of his essays about the process of "connecting and disconnecting" that is often involved in our coming to understand some new phenomenon that is before us.[20] We may initially and unreflectively place the new object or event into the wrong context of interpretation and misconstrue it, even to the point of misperceiving it. The object or event may resist our misconstrual or misperception more or less successfully, creating problems in several dimensions of our psyche, but often it is not until another context of interpretation occurs to us (or is presented to us) that we are able to reconstrue the reality. At least in some realms of experience, this process of connecting, disconnecting, and reconnecting must go on indefinitely in a continuing dialectic.[21] In another essay, Wisdom offers this memorable illustration: Mr. Flood, a zookeeper at the Dublin Zoo who had a remarkable record of achievement at the difficult task of breeding lions in captivity, was interviewed one day by a newspaper reporter. "Asked the secret of his success, Mr. Flood replied, 'Understanding lions.' Asked in what consists the understanding of lions, he replied, 'Every lion is different.'"[22]

V.

Cultivating Discernment in Ministry

T he question that regularly confronts individual Christians, Christian congregations, and those in various kinds of ministerial leadership is this: How is Christian witness to be fittingly enacted in this situation? In responding to this question, we are engaging in practical theology. Practical theology is to be understood as a particular aspect of theological reflection, informed by and informing its other aspects, and not as an independent, self-contained pursuit. Practical theology is not merely a collective term for the functional specialties of clerical leadership (homiletics, pastoral care, and so forth); rather, these are best understood as particular emphases within a much broader field of inquiry into the exercise of Christian ministry—ministry which is the vocation of all Christians, individually and corporately. Practical theology is that aspect of theological inquiry that attends particularly to the question of how the Christian witness is best realized in a given context.

Learning to engage in practical theology, like learning any part of theological discipline, is not just a matter of mastering a technique. It involves becoming deeply capacitated in certain ways. In particular, it involves acquiring the knowledge—including the self-knowledge—and the abilities and qualities of mind, heart, and spirit requisite to the theological discernment of situations and of incidents in them. The need for discernment is not confined to practical theology. It is exercised throughout our theological inquiry, in our attention to biblical texts and doctrinal concepts, for example, as well as in our attention to the particular present situations that require our Christian response.

As with other aspects of theological work, gaining practical theological discernment involves some serious personal growth. This takes time and practice. In his lucid and helpful treatment of pastoral ethics, the Roman Catholic ethicist Richard M. Gula puts the point well: "In the gospel of Matthew, Jesus, who is the New Covenant, teaches that the whole Law of Moses and the teachings of the prophets can be summarized in the Great Commandment of love (Matthew 22:37-40). But to know what love demands and where to draw the line that separates loving from unloving behavior in ministerial relationships requires the demanding task of moral discernment and the vision and sensitivity of a virtuous person."[23]

Case study has been found to be a useful kind of pedagogy for practical theology, whether undertaken alone or in a group, in an academic setting or in the field. Different contexts have different strengths and drawbacks, and there is not necessarily any one "best" setting for or approach to case study. Nor is there necessarily any one "best" kind of case. In some ways, the most important and potentially the most instructive cases, or instances of practice, from which to learn are incidents in one's own experience. There is evidence of this in the ongoing use of "verbatims"—unvarnished written recollections of incidents of one's own practice—in various kinds of professional training, including education for Christian ministry. But studying cases in which one has not been directly involved also has a number of benefits.

There are clear advantages in reflecting on situations in which we are, or have been, personally involved. For instance, we normally have a more intimate and detailed knowledge of the situation from firsthand experience, helping us attain what the philosopher Gilbert Ryle called a "thick description" of it,[24] especially when it comes to our own feelings and thoughts. Because the "case" in our own experience comes not as an isolated unit but embedded in a larger context of experience, over time we may detect patterns (helpful or otherwise) in our own approach and response to situations. There is also the likelihood that reflection on our own experience will yield insights useful to our own future practice in similar situations.

There are also clear advantages in reflecting on cases outside one's own experience. Efficiency comes to mind: learning always and only by experience can be costly in several ways. There is also the fact that less personal investment may mean clearer perception with less defensiveness and rationalization. (The prophet Nathan, one suspects, may have had a reason for adopting the approach he did in his conversation with David in 2 Samuel 12.) Working with cases from elsewhere can also mean a broadening of horizons beyond one's own sphere of experience, leading to new insights.

A great deal depends upon how a case is approached. A stance of receptivity to what the case may teach is essential. Being genuinely open to learning is often risky, and our knowledge of that risk and of our instinct to avoid it may help us realize that it is important to cultivate that receptivity rather than merely trust ourselves to see things clearly. Remember Luther's observation that prayer is the first element in theology. It is not a bad idea to take this quite literally and to begin one's work on a case with prayer.

Also vital to the quality of our learning from a case are the questions we put to ourselves concerning the case. It is useful to have a pattern of inquiry thought out and followed—allowing, of course, for adjustments along the way as the inquiry develops. We want to suggest here a possible pattern of inquiry to be tried out on the situations and incidents described in the cases that constitute part 2 of this book. The pattern has some evident relation to the understanding of theological reflection that has been sketched above. This is a sort of baseline model to be adapted and refined as the reader's needs, interests, and experience may warrant.

During the Second World War, a group of prominent American theologians and ethicists was commissioned by the Federal Council of Churches to study "the relation of the church to the war in the light of the Christian faith," and to produce a report that might be useful to the churches on this subject.[25] The report of this commission, published late in 1944, is significant both in substance and in method. For our immediate purposes, it is the method that is of greatest interest. The report is divided into three sections. The first, "diagnostic" section consisted in an extended analysis of the situation: what conditions had led to the war, what was happening in and as a result of the conflict, and so forth. The diagnostic section also included an account of the difficulties that the war posed for Christians themselves in their attempts to understand and to respond to it. This was followed by a "doctrinal" section, described as "a statement of those primary Christian affirmations that seem to us normative for any attempt to deal with the problems of the Church in wartime." Here, the authors of the report attempted to identify principles

21

that would enable one to understand and respond to the situation in a way that accorded with the Christian message. The third, "practical" section of the report, then, drew on the first and second to offer a consideration of some appropriate Christian responses to the situation. (It is instructive that the report did not set forth *the* Christian response, as though there could be only one. Rather, it offers "a summary of the attitudes that seem to us to accord best with [Christian] faith in our own day and for the near future.")

The three interrelated phases of this inquiry bear a strong resemblance to those three elements of theological study that Martin Luther identified as essential: prayer, meditation, and testing. In adopting and pursuing this pattern, the report illustrates a useful triad of questions to be posed to a situation, or to a case, when it is being approached from the standpoint of practical theology:

What is going on in this situation?

How is God involved in what is going on?

What is a fitting response to what is going on?

These questions may be developed in more detail as the nature of the inquiry and the character of the situation seem to require. The questions need not be taken in order, nor separately. They represent ways of focusing attention, not independent steps in an investigation. The third question may often be the best starting point to gain some preliminary clarity as to the sort of development that is needed. For instance, nearly every case will involve a number of "actors." To deal with the third question, we may want to specify the agent or agents whose "fitting response" to the situation is at issue. The case itself may make this unmistakably obvious, but often we will have some latitude in deciding about this.

We may also need to decide what sort of "fitting response" we are interested in exploring. One way to approach this, useful particularly when considering instances involving pastoral leadership, is to ask what sort of response would best exemplify the church's ministry of Word, Sacrament, and Order in this situation.

Word: What response would best serve the truth in this situation? How is truth being evaded, distorted, or denied in what is going on? What truth needs to be told and recognized? How might Christian ministry here make manifest the prophetic work of the one who is the Truth?

Sacrament: What response would serve to overcome fault in this situation—both the "fault" of wrongdoing and the "fault" or rupture of relationships that is both consequence and cause of our misdoings? How might Christian ministry here make manifest the priestly, reconciling work of the one who is the Way?

Order: What would best serve creaturely flourishing and well-being in this situation? What response to what is going on would be in accord with God's freeing, empowering, and life-giving involvement? How might Christian ministry here make manifest the redeeming work of the one who is the Life?

It might well be that, in a given situation, one or another of these aspects of ministry is called to the fore as most needful under the circumstances; but it would be a rare instance in which all three are not *somehow* involved, and mutually implicated.

Pursuing such lines of thought as a way of opening up the third in our original triad of questions will help us focus the first two questions in the triad as well. For example, it will point us toward some things to consider, or some frames of reference for considering them, in relation to the first question. *What is going on?* might, in principle, be answered with "Well, let's see: the grass is growing, the planets are revolving in their orbits...." All this may be quite true and vitally important, but only remotely relevant to the issues of the case. (There might, of course, also be an instance in which the fact that the grass is growing is the single most pertinent fact to which our attention needs to be directed.) Our reflection needs to focus on the specific events and interactions occupying center stage in our construal of the case, without losing sight of the larger patterns of events and interactions that provide their context.

Some provisional clarity on all these points may also help us think more specifically about the second question, "Where is God in this situation?" In Jeremiah 2:4-8, the word from the Lord that the prophet conveys indicates that it is the people's (and their leaders') now-habitual failure to ask "Where is the Lord?" that is at the root of their difficulties. They have forgotten how to pay attention to God, and thus "they have forsaken me, the fountain of living water, and dug out cisterns for themselves, cracked cisterns that can hold no water" (Jeremiah 2:13). Theological discernment involves asking, "Where is the Lord?"

In approaching this central theological question, it might be well to keep in mind the ways that God may be involved in things. Treatments of the Christian doctrine of providence often distinguish among God's sustaining, governing, and cooperating work (*conservatio, gubernatio,* and *concursus*) as three aspects of God's involvement in what happens, and this or some other such reminder of the scope of divine action may be

23

useful in case analysis. In their own rendition of this threefold involvement, the authors of the Calhoun Report indicate that in whatever is
going on, God is graciously providing and sustaining the conditions for
creaturely life and fulfillment—conditions which themselves introduce
limits as well as possibilities; God is enacting judgment and mercy in
response to our doings and misdoings; and God is life-giving power.
We offer these points not as a template to be "applied" to situations,
whether real or hypothetical, but rather to suggest that ministerial leaders and ordinary Christians who have acquired the *habitus* of discernment
will tend not to overlook the richness and complexity of the "God-
relatedness" of situations.

When one is dealing with a case in one's own experience, each of our
three leading questions is already "self-involving" in that one is already a
part of the situation being described. In dealing with a case that is not
part of one's own experience, it is important pedagogically to find an
appropriate way to allow the case to address oneself. In either situation,
it is vital to recognize the issues for self-understanding as well as for
responsible handling of the case that arise, and to deal with those issues
constructively. One way to facilitate this kind of encounter is to pose a
set of questions parallel to those in our initial triad, and to make their
consideration a part of the agenda for reflection and discussion:

What is going on with you as you consider this case?

How is God involved in what is going on with you in this process?

How might you respond to what is going on with you?

Matters of ministerial practice and matters of ministerial "being" are
closely related. Who we are, and how we have become who we are,
greatly affects how we see things and how we are at least at first inclined
to behave toward things. In practicing discernment through case study, it
is natural and desirable that these connections be brought to the surface
to be recognized and addressed. The reader's analysis of the situation presented in the case will normally lead to, or even directly involve, questions touching on his or her own identity and vocation, as well as
questions having to do with what is going on in the situation and what
might constitute an appropriate response to it. These personal dimensions of the exercise are not distractions, but are instead integral to the
process of theological growth.

PART TWO

INCIDENTS AND SITUATIONS

V I .

Learning Theology Through Case Study

As the saying has it, life is what happens when you are making other plans. Christian ministry is often that way as well. The cases presented here deal mainly with everyday life in unremarkable settings—not, for the most part, with the sorts of things that one might ideally imagine church leadership to be all about but rather with the sorts of things that pastors and others in positions of responsibility often find themselves involved in day to day: teaching, leading worship, counseling, planning, to be sure, but also interruptions, distractions, detours, and obstacles. To invoke another contemporary proverb, God is in the details.

The cases that follow are not arranged in any thematic or topical order. What each case is "about," and what issues for theology and ministry it raises, are open questions, and furthermore are questions whose answer rightly depends in part upon the reader. Our hope is that, taken together, they will prove to have a fairly comprehensive range. Earlier cases in the collection may be a little easier to get into and to get hold of than later ones, although that difference, too, is relative and variable.

Here are a few suggestions on reading cases. Read the case slowly and meditatively. After a short break, read it again, soaking up detail and checking your initial perceptions of the characters and circumstances involved. Then, take some soundings in your own reception of what you have read: What is going on with you as you consider this case? What feelings, recollections, associations does it evoke in you? On that basis, make a provisional decision as to which of the two triads of questions to start with. You may think it best to begin with the second triad if the case has engaged you strongly at a personal level, so as to do some work there before proceeding to the first triad. If the case does not appear to be particularly "existential" for you in that way, however, you might begin with the first triad and then see whether your discoveries there lead to any further explorations in the personal realm. Whatever your choice, deal with the three questions of the set in whatever order seems to commend itself (e.g., moving from what is going on to what should be done, or from an intuitive sense of what should be done back to what is going on). Move on, eventually, to the other triad. Make some notes as you proceed. Wrestle with the case at various levels, or with various aspects of your being. Think about what it is doing to you, and why, and about how to use that knowledge. Be receptive, reflective, and responsive. Pursue, in imagination, one or more resolutions or further developments of the case situation.

If you are working with these cases in a group setting, some of these decisions as to how to proceed will need to be made collectively, or by a group leader, for the sake of reasonably coherent discussion. The same general principles and recommendations will apply either way. The group may have its own agenda and purposes in case study, of course, which may properly take precedence over these suggestions.

If you are dealing with these cases in a structured setting such as a class or peer group, and one of the expectations is that participants will have worked out some understanding of the case in writing in advance of the meeting, there is a set of questions adapted from the foregoing scheme that we have found very useful in such settings. It combines and develops key elements from the two triads in a way that has proven effective both in guiding written reflection and in opening up productive discussion, and so we commend it for consideration:

What is going on here? (Consider not just the specific events and interactions occupying center stage in the case, but also the larger patterns of events and interactions that provide their context.) How is God involved here? What are the theological issues?

How would you begin to deal with this situation? What resolution (or further development) of the case would seem to you most appropriate?

What is going on *with you* as you read this case, and how is God involved *with you* as you deal with this case?

For each participant to address these questions individually in three to four pages of thoughtful writing beforehand will make for a much richer and more effective discussion.

Most of the incidents and situations collected here are given a generic Protestant or ecumenical context rather than being explicitly tied to a particular denomination or tradition. Although the organizational structure of congregations varies from denomination to denomination, most mainline groups expect a relatively high level of lay participation and direction for the congregation, which operates under the leadership of an elected governing board or council. There is usually a group of laity charged with making some decisions about how worship will occur (a Worship Committee), another with some responsibilities in connection with the church's property (a Board of Trustees), and another handling personnel issues involving the pastor and other persons on the congregation's paid staff (a Staff-Parish Relations Committee). This is the nomenclature used in these cases, but readers should be able to recognize the corresponding structures within their own congregations and polities, and make any changes necessary to make the cases applicable.

Four of the cases are identified with United Methodist settings, usually so as to allow some specification in polity or doctrine that is germane to the incident described. A brief consideration of the role these specifications play within the case should help a reader from another context to make any adaptations that might be necessary in order to relate the case to his or her own experience.

VII.

"What Should We Do About Henry?"

S andra Owens had just been appointed to Redeemer, a mostly white, middle-class congregation with an average of thirty-five in worship. The church was in a large city, but not in or near the inner city. The building was bordered on three sides by businesses, with a small residential neighborhood across the street. The sanctuary would seat only about seventy comfortably, and in its forty-year history there had been only one or two years when the church had had a regular attendance that approached that number. This was in large part due to the church's very poor location. It was hidden away, hard to find, in a neighborhood cut off from most of the city by highways and other barriers, and in an area with much more commercial than residential development. Further, a much larger church of its denomination was just a few miles away.

When the chair of the Staff-Parish Relations (SPR) Committee called to welcome her to Redeemer and invite her to a get-acquainted meeting with some of its members, she told Sandra, "Now, one thing I need to tell you about is Henry. Henry is a homeless man who's sort of adopted our church—or we've adopted him—anyway, he lives outside. When you drive up, he may be outside the building, so don't be startled. He's harmless."

When Sandra attended that meeting, Henry was not at the church, but was off on one of his daily excursions around the neighborhood, seeking food, visiting with other homeless friends, or who knows what. After the main meeting, the SPR chair and the chair of the Administrative Council had a private conversation with Sandra, and one topic that came up was Henry. It turned out that there was a good deal of dissension among the membership (and disagreement between those two important leaders) about him. They said that several months previously, on a week-day, there had been a small fire in a Sunday school room. Some members blamed Henry for setting it, while others credited him with having saved the building by scaring off intruders who had set it. Some members were convinced that Henry helped keep vandalism to a minimum by scaring or warning off neighborhood youngsters who might do damage. Others felt that Henry himself was a source of damage.

The pastor Sandra replaced had had a nervous breakdown and taken early retirement, and did not provide the kind of background information that a new pastor might expect to receive from a colleague. In their one brief conversation, he simply stated that there were differing opinions about Henry among the congregation and commented on what an annoy-ance the messages Henry left on the church's answering machine had been. He refused to state any opinion about Henry's potential for vio-lence or whether Henry should be allowed to live at the church. When Sandra brought the matter up in her next conversation with the regional executive, he merely agreed that it was a key component in the church's many problems. He and Sandra both knew that the congregation had a high hostility level and a reputation as being hard to pastor, and that most ministers who had served it had left the local pastorate before too long. He offered no suggestions or support.

Sandra's first Administrative Council meeting occurred just a couple of weeks after she arrived. The board wanted Sandra's opinion on what they should do about Henry, and she got the impression that they were hoping she would tell them authoritatively what to do. She stated that while she was a firm believer in the church's responsibility to those who needed help, including the homeless, she did not know enough yet about this particular, obviously complicated, situation to offer an opinion. She asked for time, until the next board meeting (which would be held in about two months), to investigate and to reflect.

Because Henry was often gone when Sandra was at the church, her encounters with him were limited; in fact, he seemed to go out of his way to avoid her. She was, however, able to form an opinion of him through the long, rambling telephone messages her predecessor had mentioned. When she first accessed the church's voice mail, she thought she must be listening to several weeks' worth of messages, but she soon realized they could easily have been the product of one or two days. Only one or two members had ever heard any of the messages, since only the pastor had the access code, but everyone had heard the former pastor's complaints about them. Both the content and the way the messages were phrased and delivered convinced Sandra that while Henry was able to function on some levels, he suffered from a serious mental illness.

Sandra began a program of visitation with all the church members, and she asked most of them how they felt about Henry and what their experiences with him had been. As facts came to light, she pieced together a picture of his history with Redeemer.

Henry had already been a homeless person for some time when he began attending the church about two years previously. He attended faithfully each week. Over time, the church began to pay him $10 per week to pick up paper and trash out of the yard. He, in turn, put a small amount in the collection plate each week.

When the church constructed a platform outside a side door to the facility to make that entrance easier to use, Henry immediately moved his belongings onto it and began to live there under a tarpaulin he used as a tent. Since he lived outside without bathing facilities, Henry's body odor had soon become an issue, especially among the fastidious elderly women near whom he sat. A few members volunteered to take his clothes home and wash them to try to alleviate the problem, and at least one member was continuing to do his laundry once a week when Sandra arrived.

By then, however, his odor was no longer a problem in worship. Henry had stopped attending services some months before as a result of a change in the sanctuary—the denomination's logo had been added to the wall behind the communion table. Henry told the members that they had become "idolaters" because they had placed symbols inside the church. He also identified "idolatrous" symbols elsewhere; for instance, he told the choir director that the fish symbol on his Bible cover made him an idolater. He said that he would no longer enter the building lest he become an idolater, as well.

Nevertheless, this assertion did not convince those members who thought he could gain access to the building in their absence, and they still thought that it was he who was responsible for the disappearance of various small items (including one of Sandra's Bibles, which she left in the pulpit for use there). Sandra and others who came to the church during the week frequently found outside doors unlocked, even though they, and Sandra, were sure the doors had been locked securely after services on Sunday.

Along with the $10 a week the church paid Henry for picking up trash, a number of members brought him food on a regular basis. One, a single woman in her late sixties, said that some months previously, on a night that was unusually cold for their Southern city, she became concerned about Henry and brought him an extra blanket. She found that he had candles burning under the tarpaulin, presumably for extra warmth. She told him this was unsafe, but he did not extinguish them, and she was terrified all that night that there would be a fire that would injure or kill Henry, and possibly destroy the church and the buildings that were immediately adjacent to it as well. She had felt helpless to prevent a disaster that night, and she was still concerned that the incident would be repeated.

The member who felt the most responsibility for the safety of the building, along with the legal and/or insurance concerns that accompanied a homeless person inhabiting the yard, was Sam, the chair of the Board of Trustees. Fortunately for Sandra, Sam was not just a competent and capable individual who had retired from an executive position involving plant maintenance, but also a kind man with a calming presence who rarely got upset. He told Sandra that he had made numerous attempts to get Henry to seek the various forms of assistance and services that were available for the homeless, but that Henry consistently refused. "When I told him I'd try to help him get Social Security disability, he told me he had a million and a half dollars in the bank and that he didn't need any money," Sam recalled. "And maybe he does have money and just chooses to live like this—but whether he does or not, I still can't make him let me help him."

Sam's and other members' attempts to find out about Henry's family had always led to dead ends, and the telephone messages Henry left included occasional mention of how unfairly he had been treated when his wife "took him to court" for a divorce. His speech patterns indicated some non-Southern origin, and his messages mentioned a past career in the Merchant Marine and travels all over the globe—but he also talked about careers in the Army, the Navy, the Marine Corps, and the CIA, so any accurate clues about his origins remained buried amid thousands of bits of inaccurate and self-contradictory data. "Even if we could find his family," Sam said, "there's no reason to think they'd be able to make him accept help any more than we can."

It was also Sam who first articulated to Sandra what most, if not all, the members thought about the prospect of increasing, rather than decreasing, their involvement with Henry: "We can't let him live inside, because he would soon have other homeless people in there with him. He's mentally ill, and we can't predict what he might do, much less what people we don't even know might do. Our own people would be afraid to come inside, night or day." And, he said to Sandra, "I've always had a decent relationship with Henry, and if you think he needs to leave, I'll be happy to be the one to tell him."

Because of Sandra's own long commitment to social justice, she had good contacts among people involved in social service agencies, and she felt that she was as well positioned as anyone to find services that might be available to assist Henry. She spent considerable time exploring those options; however, her investigations revealed only that there was no agency in that locality that could or would force Henry to stay in a shelter or hospital if he did not wish to do so. Even the police said they would be happy to tell Henry he had to "move along," but this would merely result in his living outdoors in a different location, and possibly one not as safe or comfortable for him as the platform outside Redeemer.

As the next few weeks passed, Sandra noticed that while the tone of Henry's telephone messages remained constant, the content began to change. His purchases with the $10 he earned included batteries for a radio that he kept with him constantly. He preferred religious programming offered by radio evangelists and very conservative institutions that emphasized "family values," and the messages began to include negative comments, which he said were quotations from radio preachers, about the women's liberation movement. He maintained that women in the workforce (instead of at home where they belonged) were "the cause of all the country's problems." He began to talk frequently about witches and to accuse the congregation of practicing witchcraft because he had once visited a Shinto temple that had trees in its yard, and the church also had trees in its yard—but the primary reason, Sandra was sure, was that she was an ordained female.

He frequently read passages from the Hebrew Scriptures, and the context made it clear that he believed its injunctions were to be taken quite literally by Christians today. Sandra knew that if he had not encountered the injunction that a witch should not be allowed to live, it was just a matter of time before he did.

At the same time that she was becoming more concerned about Henry, Sandra was also becoming better acquainted with the dynamics of the congregation and aware of other conflicts bubbling not far beneath the surface. She began to think that it was possible that certain members, including some troubled teens, were at least as likely to be responsible for the fire and petty thefts as Henry was.

She knew that her hard-earned reputation as an advocate for social justice would suffer if word spread that she had dealt unfairly with a homeless individual at her own church; and on a more basic level, her ability to address social justice issues from the pulpit, as she frequently did, would suffer if she felt that she had sacrificed her own integrity on the issue.

The time for the next council meeting was approaching, and Sandra knew that it was inevitable that the question would be raised again: "What should we do about Henry?" This time, she would have to have some sort of answer.

VIII.

Help Thou His Unbelief

Bob had been pastor at St. Miscellaneous United Methodist Church for five years and had grown to know the active members well. There were, as is the case in most churches, some who had joined St. Misc as children or youth and who had never moved their membership elsewhere, and who were still connected to St. Misc through relatives who were active in the church. He was not that well acquainted with most of those members.

Among the active members at St. Misc were the Robinsons. The oldest generation was a couple now in their seventies who were dyed-in-the-wool Methodists and who had represented the congregation at Annual Conference many times and served in many leadership roles over the decades. Relationships with them were not always smooth, however. Linda and Jerome had left and returned to the church several times, as they got angry at a pastor for one reason or another and went off to attend a different Methodist church until the offending pastor left. Linda in particular took her faith very seriously, and was dedicated to doing what she believed was right, but she had a very rigid definition of acceptable Christian behavior and tended to treat other members judgmentally. She and Jerome had disagreed with several of Bob's views and policies, but they had never stopped attending during his tenure there.

The Robinsons had several children, but all except one had moved away to other states, a fact that Bob did not find surprising. One daughter and her family still lived nearby, and they were active in the congregation.

Although Linda and Jerome's son Joshua had moved away, Joshua's son, Kevin, who was now in his twenties, still lived near St. Misc. Though he was a member, having been confirmed at around age twelve, Kevin attended St. Misc only on very rare occasions—a funeral, a family wedding, or a service in which his grandparents were particularly involved in some way. He had never had much to say to the pastor, and Bob did not feel that he really knew him. When Kevin had married two years earlier, the wedding was held in his wife's family's church, which was affiliated with another denomination.

In recent months, Linda and Jerome had used the "Joys and Concerns" segment of the worship service to rejoice over the impending and then the actual birth of their first great-grandchild, Emma, the daughter of Kevin and his wife, Kimberly. Emma had not actually appeared at St. Misc, which was not surprising, given the extremely sporadic attendance record of her parents.

One Wednesday morning before Bible study, Linda approached Bob to tell him that Kevin and Kimberly wanted to have Emma baptized at St. Misc on a particular Sunday about four weeks away. She was obviously delighted with this decision (in which Bob suspected she had played an integral role); indeed, he had never seen her so happy. Bob explained that the parents would have to come in for a session of instruction, which did not seem to come as a surprise to Linda. She tried to set up a time with him when they could come, but he gently insisted that the couple themselves should contact him. Although he did not articulate it, he always had a less-than-joyous response to requests to baptize babies when he felt almost certain that the parents would not be an active part of the congregation after the baptism. He felt that the least the parents could do was to initiate an appointment themselves, and that their doing so represented a modicum of assumption of responsibility for their child's spiritual upbringing.

In a few days, Kevin did call and set up an appointment for about a week later, but when the day came, he and Kimberly did not show up. Instead, Bob received a call from Linda, explaining that Kevin "had been held up" and promising that he would call to reschedule. In a few days, he did call, and the appointment was set again. This time, Kevin, Kimberly, and Emma all appeared in Bob's office.

After a few moments of small talk and admiring the new baby, Bob turned the conversation to the upcoming baptism. Immediately, Kevin broke in. "I need to tell you upfront," he said, "I'm just doing this for my grandparents. I'm an atheist myself."

"Well," replied Bob, "that could present some problems, since you as parents are asked to express your faith as Christians as part of the ritual. We'll definitely need to talk about this more." After some clarifying questions and responses, Bob realized, and said, that Kevin was not really an atheist, but rather an agnostic.

Kevin seemed comfortable with that label. Still, that did not really solve what Bob viewed as the problem with conducting a ritual that would ask Kevin to affirm a faith in Christ that Kevin clearly did not possess. Further, Bob explained to the couple that along with affirming their own faith, they would also promise to raise the baby in the church, so that she would receive Christian instruction.

"Asking you to take vows that I know you don't mean is really problematic for me. Do you understand what it means for a lawyer to suborn perjury?" he asked. Kevin said that he did. "I feel as though I'd be arranging for you to lie, not to a human court, but directly to God," he said. Kevin said that it made no difference to him, since he doubted that God existed anyway.

Kimberly, on the other hand, expressed a willingness to move her membership from her childhood church and become a formal member at St. Misc. She said she would have no difficulty in expressing the beliefs of the Apostles' Creed, and that she would be willing to promise to raise Emma in the church. Bob did not have any reason to think that she was more likely to follow through on providing Christian instruction for Emma than a number of other parents whose children he had baptized and who had never shown up at church again had proved to be. However, he also had no reason to doubt the validity of her expression of faith in Christ, and would probably not have been overly concerned about her responses had her husband not begun the session by declaring himself an atheist.

"This is clearly a situation where we need more sessions before the baptism itself," Bob said. "How does Saturday afternoon look for the two of you?"

Kevin immediately objected, offering reasons he could not return soon for more sessions, and when Bob stated that the baptism would therefore need to be postponed, he objected strenuously. "This is for my grandparents, anyway," he said, "and they've already planned a big party and rented a hall and my aunts and uncles have bought plane tickets to come in. And I don't see what good more sessions will do; I've thought about religion a lot, and you're not going to make me believe in God in the next few weeks, anyway."

"I need to think for a moment," Bob said, and he got up and left the office. Standing outside in the hall, he tried to imagine what the ritual would be like if he conducted it. He could see the grandparents and other sponsors standing around the baby and the couple, and he could imagine the mother and many of the other respondents answering with what he would have to presume was honesty about their Christian beliefs and intentions. He could also see the crisis and conflict in the church that would inevitably ensue if he refused to baptize Emma on the Sunday the family had chosen.

He recalled that he had actually had some objections to infant baptism when he began the process toward ordination in the UMC, and that he had studied the issue quite carefully during his seminary studies. He had come to believe quite sincerely that infants could be baptized because it was God's gift of grace that the ritual celebrated, and that this could occur even if the baptisand was not old enough to participate fully in the rite.

Further, Bob remembered that there had been a pastor in his Annual Conference who had been appointed to a small rural location in a predominantly Roman Catholic area where his predecessors at the Methodist church performed infant baptisms that the local priest had refused to perform because the parents could not be married in the Catholic Church. Since most Roman Catholics in that area believed that babies would not be admitted to heaven if they died before they were baptized, it seemed a real kindness to the parents to perform the baptisms. When Bob's acquaintance was appointed to that church, he stopped such baptisms, because he also believed the baby's parents had to be married in order to have their child receive the baptismal waters. Bob had regarded this as mean-spirited and theologically in error. Now, he wondered whether refusing to baptize Emma because Kevin was not a Christian wouldn't be denying the grace of God to the baby and the rest of her family in much the same way that he felt the other pastor's refusal had done.

Bob closed his eyes and prayed for guidance and clarity of mind as he struggled to decide what to say to the young couple.

Paying Your Dues

Maribeth Silver, an ordained elder in The United Methodist Church, was assigned as mentor to a brand new pastor, Judith Tolbert. In their initial conversations, Maribeth learned that Judith had received her religious training as a child in Catholic schools, and that she had spent a good bit of her adult life outside the organized church. Now a middle-aged woman, Judith had come to United Methodism fairly late in life, and before she answered her call to attend seminary, she had attended only one congregation.

After years of study and preparation, Judith had been appointed as pastor of a small congregation. Her fourth Sunday there was a Communion Sunday, and as she celebrated the sacrament for the first time, her parishioners came to kneel at the chancel rail as they were accustomed to doing. In the one United Methodist congregation Judith had regularly attended, communion had always been served by intinction, while the parishioners stood. In her Roman Catholic childhood, she had also received the Eucharist while standing. She had attended an ecumenical seminary and had gone all the way through the process of being commissioned as a probationary elder without ever having spent any significant time in a congregation where the tradition for the serving of the Eucharist was to kneel at the altar rail to receive the elements. Thus, serving communion for the first time was a new experience for her in several different ways.

Maribeth had scheduled a lunch with Judith that week to check on how her first month in the pulpit had been. Overall, Judith was able to report that things were going well and that she was very happy in her new position. However, one occurrence had left her aghast, and she told Maribeth that she had immediately instituted a change in that area.

"They were leaving money on the rail when they came for communion!" she reported, still shaking her head in disbelief. "It was barbaric—they've been paying for communion!"

Maribeth bit her lip and managed not to laugh. "Um—that's what we call a 'communion offering,'" she said. "Lots of churches—probably most churches—do that, and it's voluntary. People don't think of it as paying for communion—it's just a way to collect an offering for some special purpose. Some pastors use it for the special offerings that we're to take every year, or for a pastor's discretionary fund; there are all sorts of ways you can use the money. And when you say you changed it—do you mean you said they couldn't make the offering anymore?"

Judith replied that she had tried to get them to suspend the offering, but when they objected, she told them that they could put baskets out in some other location. "I didn't like that," she said, "but at least there won't be such a close connection between paying and receiving the bread and wine." And, while Judith didn't say so directly, Maribeth could see that what she had said so far about the offering had not convinced Judith herself that it wasn't the same as paying to partake of the sacrament.

Maribeth remembered that in her first appointment, which was her internship for seminary, she had faced a situation that had seemed as strange to her as the offering on the rail seemed to Judith. She told Judith about her internship, where she had served a black congregation as their first white pastor. One of her regular duties was to deliver communion to each of the church's many shut-in members, and despite the time it required, she found that it was one of the most enjoyable tasks of her ministry there. She learned a tremendous amount about pastoring and about how laypeople did theology, and she had used those encounters as the basis for several of the reflection papers that she had to write for her intern supervisor. One of those papers had focused on the one negative aspect of delivering communion—the fact that this particular congregation expected her to "collect the dues" of the shut-ins while she was there.

The congregation had been in place for many decades, and all its customs were deeply entrenched. Maribeth had never ascertained whether there was an elaborate system for deciding how much each family should pay, based on their resources, as she thought was the case in many Jewish synagogues, or whether each family was required to pledge a particular amount of their choosing each year. What was quite clear to her was that however the amount was determined, each member was expected to pay it, and pay it regularly, if they wished to be considered "in good standing" with the rest of the church. Whenever an individual or a couple were not able to pay, they tended to be uncomfortable about her presence and about receiving communion, although she assured them repeatedly that the two things were not linked. One couple who fell way behind during her tenure at the church actually began to pretend they weren't home when she arrived, leaving her standing on the step with the communion set while they ignored her knocks. When their financial circumstances improved, they invited her in happily, gave her an envelope to take to the treasurer, and took communion with evident joy. Once again, she assured them that receiving communion was not linked to the payment she was taking, and they nodded agreement, but she nevertheless felt that she hadn't "gotten through" with the message.

She and her own mentor had discussed the reflection paper she wrote about the incident, and had come to the conclusions that it was part of a cultural heritage that they could not quite grasp because they were both white, and that it was not appropriate for them to attempt to judge it or try to change it, particularly because her internship-length appointment would be ending in just a few months. Although Maribeth had continued to deliver communion and to take envelopes back to the treasurer for the rest of her pastorate there without ever raising the issue with the congregation, she never felt quite comfortable about that process.

Now, as she and Judith discussed that experience in the light of Judith's new observation, she began to see that she had simply never questioned the practice of putting money on the communion rail or its possible linkage to receiving communion in the minds of some or all parishioners, simply because it was a part of her own cultural heritage. It felt familiar and "okay" to her because she had been exposed to the practice all her life, but perhaps it was in fact as questionable as the customary "dues paying" at the black church had seemed to her. Certainly, Judith felt that way. Maribeth was struck once again with the difficulty of separating Christian practice and cultural practice, and wondered whether the communion offering was truly as harmless as she supposed, or whether it wouldn't be fruitful to do more theological reflection on the issue. Further, she wondered how congregations like Judith's would respond if they were told that their established way of collecting funds for certain purposes was theologically suspect and that they should find a different way to raise the money instead.

Food + Money = Food Bank

After concentrating on urban ministry during his seminary studies, Ken Ballard was thrilled that his first position as a minister was to be in an inner city setting. He was sent to the Mt. Zion congregation, located in what had been the heart of the African-American section of a city of about 100,000. Because of the sites chosen for interstates, other major roads and highways, and the civic center and city government complexes, the once thriving neighborhood had been split into many sections. The area immediately surrounding the church building had deteriorated into a mix of light commercial activity and housing of not much more than slum caliber. Drug dealers, streetwalkers, and gangs all operated in the same block as the church.

Mt. Zion's structure had at one time been grand, back when the congregation was composed of doctors, lawyers, educators, and other professional members of the African-American community. Now, most of those individuals had moved far from the city center and were no longer part of the congregation. The impressive sanctuary held only fifteen to twenty worshippers on Sunday mornings, with almost all of those aged sixty-five or older. The tiny group struggled to keep the church financially afloat.

The building itself had fallen into extreme disrepair, and it was a frequent target for robberies, as addicts searched for funds to buy the drugs that were readily available on nearby corners. All of the altar and Communion ware, along with furniture that was not too heavy to haul out, had been stolen, and anything replaced had been stolen again. A less expensive cross and candlesticks were now in use, and one of the members carried them home after service each week to prevent their being stolen, too.

Rather than assisting Mt. Zion, the church hierarchy had put resources into a new church starting in a cross-town neighborhood where middle-class black families still resided, and some of the membership from Mt. Zion had moved to that congregation. It seemed to Ken that most people had simply given up on Mt. Zion. While he was new to the area and hardly knew everything there was to know about matters, Ken tended to believe that the conference should be spending more, not less, on Mt. Zion, because it represented the church's only foothold in the inner city, and because it was precisely there where the church needed most to be in mission.

About a month after he came to the church, Ken found a bill for $191.78 in the mail from a state-wide food bank program. It was addressed to Mt. Zion, but as far as he knew the church did not have a food bank, and he thought perhaps the bill had been sent by mistake. He called the food bank, which was based in the state's capital city, to try to find out more.

He discovered that the food bank operation, sponsored by a large gro-cery store chain and aided by private contributions, furnished food for the poor to sponsoring organizations at a greatly reduced rate—just a few cents on the dollar for the worth of the food. Once a church had been selected as a distribution site, there were only a few rules by which they had to abide. An order had to be placed each week for what food was needed, someone authorized by the church had to come to a central site and collect the food at a particular day and time, and the food had to be stored in a separate location from the church's own kitchen—a different room in another part of the building would suffice. The church could dis-tribute the food to anyone they chose, in whatever manner they decided. They were required to keep fairly current on the food bill, and eventually would be cut off from supplies if they did not.

Ken also learned that Mt. Zion had indeed had a food bank that had closed about fourteen months previously when non-payment had stopped the delivery of orders, and that the food bank was still trying to collect the last amount the church owed. In reality, they were still eager to have Mt. Zion be a distribution center since there was not another one oper-ating in the city, and they hoped the bill would be paid so that they could continue to work with the congregation. He also discovered that the per-son who had been placing orders for the church was Emily Standard.

His first few weeks at Mt. Zion had already taught him that Emily Standard, a prominent member of the church, had been in conflict for decades with Mary Thomas, the chair of the administrative council and the church's prime donor. Mary had little patience with anyone who did not pull their share of the financial load. In her opinion, Emily Standard was such a person. None of the members was wealthy, but Emily appeared to be among the least well off. Ken had visited in her home, and he did not think she had any significant financial resources. Mary, on the other hand, seemed to have money for whatever she chose to do, but it was clear that she had worked hard and lived frugally in order to have it.

The administrative council met the next afternoon, and he asked about the bill at the meeting. Emily was not present, and the rest of the group quickly informed him that the bill, though addressed to the church, was not something they considered to be the church's obligation. Emily had made the agreement with the food bank without the approval of the council, they said, and had caused all sorts of problems by so doing. They were convinced that the presence of the food in the church building (indeed, in the church's kitchen, despite the rule prohibiting its storage there) was one of the reasons the church had been robbed so frequently. They were also angry because Emily, who was in her seventies, who suffered from decreased mobility, and who further did not own a van or large vehicle, often said that she couldn't go and collect the food at the appointed times, so that other members had to haul cases of food around despite their own advanced age and frailty. Overall, the program had been a source of contention throughout its existence, and none of the council was willing to have the church pay what they considered Emily's own personal obligation to the food bank. The most vocal opponent was Mary Thomas, but it appeared that others were in agreement with her assessment. Ken had already realized that most of the church's funds came from Mary, and he could see that she would have to put in extra money to pay the bill if the church were to pay it, and that she would never be persuaded to "rescue" Emily from the obligation.

The next day, Ken visited Emily Standard. Her story was, predictably, somewhat different. She felt that the church *had* agreed to participate, but nevertheless, she had been "trying" to pay off the bill herself. She would pay the bill, no matter how long it took her, she said, but she hadn't been able to put anything at all toward it in the past several months. She believed that it was uncharitable for the other members not to wish to continue participating in the food distribution, and stated that the presence of the food had not led to any of the break-ins at the church. She was sure, she said, that Ken would be able to make the other members become "more Christian" in time. The new pastor felt that when she said she would pay the bill eventually, she secretly hoped that he would tell her she did not need to do so.

After these events, Ken spent several days reflecting on the situation. He could see that Emily and Mary's long-standing rivalry was part of the problem, and he thought that both of the women had acted badly toward one another because of their own desires for power, and that they had both been in error not just in this situation, but also in many other circumstances about which he had begun to hear bits and pieces. He could see that a food bank would be a good ministry for the neighborhood, but he could also see that it was beyond the members' abilities to manage at that time, and that Emily would not, and probably could not, ever assume any more real responsibility for the program than she had in the past. He could see that the council was extremely unlikely to change its position on paying the bill, and he could see that Emily was either unwilling or unable, and possibly both, to pay it herself. He also felt that the food bank organization had been operating in good faith and had been unaware of the lack of approval of the council for the project, and that their expectation that the bill should be paid was appropriate. They operated on a shoestring budget, and it might even be the case that the church's (or Emily's) failure to pay the bill was preventing some other individuals from receiving assistance.

When Ken accepted the appointment to Mt. Zion, the denomination's regional executive, Andrew, had invited him to "check in" from time to time about any thorny problems that might arise. Ken felt that he could certainly benefit from some objective counsel on the issue, and he made an appointment for a visit. After some coffee and general conversation, he laid out the facts of the situation and asked for advice. Andrew replied, "Well, my personality is to be a 'fixer,' and I propose a 'fix.' I have some funds in the regional budget that could be applied to this. If you want me to, I'll just pay the bill, on the condition that the church not incur any more debt on this program. But my fiscal year is ending at the end of next month, so you'll have to tell me in a couple of weeks, because I need to use the money somewhere else if you don't want it for this."

During the course of his studies in urban ministry, Ken had been sensitized to the issues of empowerment and disempowerment of the poor, and he was unsure that having someone pay the bill for them would be the best thing for the church or for Emily. He also felt that the food bank deserved its money and he could see no other way to get it, but as the spiritual leader of the congregation, he felt it was somehow wrong to arrange things so that Emily (or the church, depending on which side of the story he believed) did not have to meet the responsibility she (or they) had undertaken. If Emily had truly misled the food bank into thinking she had council approval when she did not, it seemed a fairly serious matter and a misdeed that she should not be encouraged to try again. On the other hand, it seemed wrong to make a poor woman pay $191 that she did not have, especially if she had truly believed the church was responsible. He believed that having the congregation work through the problem itself would be most beneficial in the long run, but he could see that the problem between the two powerful women had been festering for many decades, and he was concerned that if he brought Mary and Emily into open conflict so early in his appointment there, it would spoil whatever chances he had for a successful ministry at Mt. Zion. He had already begun to love the parishioners and the neighborhood and to feel a vision for what the church could be about in mission to the community around it.

Ken told Andrew that he would think about his offer, and let him know soon what he decided.

Why Can't They Just Levitate?

St. Miscellaneous church was about sixty years old, and the building was beginning to need a good bit of maintenance and upkeep. The congregation had aged as well, and most of the people carried AARP cards in their wallets. Still, a number of younger families helped keep the congregation vital, and since the church was located in a suburb with higher percentages of affluent and well-educated (and therefore healthier) people than in most communities, many elderly members were still vigorous and active.

Inevitably, though, some members began to have difficulty in getting around, and making the climb to the church's second-floor choir room became harder each year for the dozen or so faithful singers. One had ruined a knee jogging, one had never recovered properly after a broken ankle, one was short of breath due to a heart condition, one was losing her eyesight, and a few had some of the general mobility issues often associated with aging. Bob usually chatted with members of the adult Sunday school class in the hall near the staircase at about the same time the choir members were heading upstairs to don their robes and go over the morning's special music, and he frequently had an opportunity to observe how the members paused to gather their strength for the climb that they clearly dreaded making.

The church had made some concessions to the needs of the disabled, installing a wheelchair ramp and some handrails at the main entrance to the sanctuary. Otherwise, though, the interior and exterior of the building were full of obstacles for those with mobility impairments. Even the one bathroom on the ground floor was not handicap accessible.

Despite the affluence of the community, many of the St. Misc members had retired and now considered themselves to be on "fixed incomes." Bob was aware that their incomes were fixed much, much higher than those of most Americans, but he nevertheless understood that most of these individuals saw themselves as being financially at risk. After two or three of the larger donors died, the church itself began to feel a financial strain, and it was a bit harder to make the budget each year. Then, a particular member who had been among the richest died and, being childless and a widow, left her entire estate to the church. When all the dust had settled, the legacy amounted to about a quarter of a million dollars. Though some of Bob's younger colleagues were envious and thought that it would solve many of their problems if something similar happened in their churches, Bob had watched dozens of families share inheritances, and he was not surprised to discover that the gift was not a healthy thing for the congregation.

He was surprised, however, to discover in exactly what way the windfall would prove to be problematic. Having envisioned fights between individuals or factions, each of whom wanted to spend the money a different way, he found instead a consensus that the money should not be spent at all. There was a great deal of talk about "good stewardship." Many were willing to articulate the idea that investing the money, spending only the interest (or perhaps only part of it), and thus keeping the principal in reserve for future "hard times" was obviously the "responsible" course to take; others simply nodded in tacit agreement with these sentiments whenever they were voiced. A very few suggested mission projects, the most ambitious of which would cost $5000.

Bob was a proponent of empowering the laity and understood well that it was vital for the congregation to "own" any project they adopted. Believing that it might help open their hearts to others, he thought that perhaps the congregation could install a handicap accessible bathroom and perhaps an elevator or chair lift to the second floor, as this would benefit their own members while making the building more hospitable to others. At the next board of trustees meeting, he mentioned the difficulty that some of the choir members were having getting upstairs and that some of the money might be used to make the church more accessible for them.

Jack, a vocal member who had crossed swords with ministers before, spoke up right away. "We have to think of the good of the whole group," he said, "and we wouldn't be good Christian stewards if we spent so much money for just a few individuals."

Bob said nothing at first, thinking that surely one of the laypeople would react to that statement, but then he realized that all the trustees, including Jack, were looking at him and waiting for a response.

XII.

A Funny Way of Showing It

Sandra had heard stories for years from pastors who insisted that they had been sent to such-and-such a church "with instructions to close it down" and had managed to breathe new life into the congregation instead. She had some doubts about the stories, not so much because she doubted that a dying congregation could be resurrected, but because it was difficult for her to imagine a regional executive admitting to a pastor that all the church she was receiving needed was some good hospice care. Thus it was with some surprise and regret that she heard her own appointment explained one year with the words, "Redeemer is dying, and they just need pastoral care till they admit that and close their doors."

Because her daughter's desire to attend a particular school had prompted her to ask for an appointment within a specific geographical area for that one year, Sandra was not taken aback by being given a less-than-completely-desirable appointment in that area. She was, however, unsure how to approach a less-than-demanding position and wondered what sort of volunteer work she might take on to fill her extra time.

As it turned out, the issue never arose. Sandra found that while the overall congregation was dwindling in numbers and perhaps indeed dying out, there were plenty of individual members whose situations were prompting them to grapple with complex theological issues. In fact, some of her parishioners' questions required her to draw on every bit of theological expertise she possessed and sometimes sent her back to her seminary textbooks for extra help. One of the people posing those difficult questions was Nicole.

Nicole had appeared at Redeemer for the first time about a month after Sandra's first Sunday there. She was a single, professional woman in her mid-forties who told Sandra as she left church that first Sunday that she had been drawn to Redeemer when she noticed a woman's name on the sign that identified the pastor. "I thought it would be a different experience to hear a woman preach," she said. "I like it." Sandra asked if she would like a visit, but Nicole suggested that they have coffee at a popular café instead.

When they met there, Sandra learned that Nicole had been attending a church affiliated with a different denomination up until a couple of months before she came to Redeemer. She closed that avenue of conversation, though, when Sandra moved toward asking why she'd stopped attending there. Through things Nicole said and things she didn't say, and through nonverbal clues, Sandra was led to wonder whether Nicole had been having an affair with the man who had previously been her pastor, but it was clear that if she had, she was not inclined to talk about it.

Redeemer's congregation made Nicole as welcome as they ever did any newcomer, and she moved her church membership there after a few months. She attended worship regularly, but she didn't really find a home in the adult Sunday school class, and she didn't sing in the choir. It was clear to Sandra that much of Nicole's spiritual nourishment was coming from their coffee hours together, which they arranged two or three times a month. Nicole was eager to learn more about the Bible and the Christian faith, and when Sandra suggested books for her, she would purchase and read them quickly.

A paralegal, and apparently a very good one considering the law firm she worked for and the level of responsibility she was given there, Nicole often attempted to apply what she was learning to ethics that pertained to her job. She was careful never to violate client confidences, but she obviously enjoyed the intellectual exercise that talking about ethical matters with Sandra provided her.

When, after several months, Sandra asked whether Nicole had ever thought of going to law school herself, Nicole finally opened up a bit and told Sandra some of her story. She had married quite young to a man who had soon become abusive. Unwilling to admit that her marriage was not working out, Nicole had stayed with him and had two daughters in rapid succession. When she had begun to be concerned for the safety of her children, Nicole had finally left, but the divorce was messy and painful; her ex-husband had stalked her and she had to obtain restraining orders against him. She had never remarried. "I had some trust issues with men," she understated.

Before Nicole reached the part of the story that had brought her to the city where she now lived, and to the church she had stopped attending before she came to Redeemer, their time together was over, as Sandra had another appointment. "I hope I get a raincheck for the rest of the story," she said as she left, and Nicole assured her that she would pick up where she left off the next time they met for coffee.

The next Sunday was the first Sunday in Lent, and as Sandra was accustomed to doing, she made physical changes in the sanctuary to mark observance of the season. She draped the large, shiny cross on the wall behind the communion table with a purple cloth, and replaced the congregation's silk flower arrangement with a container full of interesting but bare branches. She also placed a crudely fashioned cross made of rough wood in a prominent position on the chancel rail.

She replaced the paraments and her stole with purple ones appropriate to the season, and during the children's sermon, she told the children (and thus the congregation) about the meaning of the liturgical color and the significance of preparing for Easter.

Throughout the service, she could see that Nicole was not as alert and involved as she usually was, but she didn't attach much significance to the observation. Late that evening, though, she received a call at home from Nicole. "I'm so sorry to call you at home so late," she said, "but I wonder if you could have breakfast with me tomorrow. I have some things I really need to talk to you about." Because of the unusual nature of the request, Sandra understood that something serious was at stake, and she agreed to the breakfast meeting.

The next morning, Nicole was waiting for her when she arrived at the coffee house. Sandra barely finished ordering before Nicole began to speak in a somewhat agitated way. "That wooden cross yesterday was so upsetting," she said. "I know I'm not supposed to be upset by it, that it's stupid. Ed made that perfectly clear to me."

She paused, and after a moment's internal debate about where to start, Sandra said, "Ed?"

"The pastor at First Avenue," Nicole explained, naming the large church from which she had recently moved. "I know you've wanted to ask about my leaving there, and I appreciate that you haven't. I don't know how to say this, but Ed and I were having an affair."

"He's married?" Sandra asked.

"Oh, yeah," Nicole replied. "He said that his wife was beginning to suspect, and that if she left him, his denomination would kick him out. He said he just couldn't give up his ministry for me. I know I should have known better all along, but he was so kind when I first went to him for counseling. That's why I chose a church with a woman pastor this time, and you've been so much more helpful about explaining the things I want to know. When I tried to talk to him about the cross, he said I was asking stupid questions."

She paused again, and once more Sandra had to decide which way to move the conversation. She chose to ask, "What is it that you found so disturbing in church yesterday?"

"Well, I just don't understand. If God is so good and so full of love, why did he make his son get nailed to a tree? I looked at that cross you put on the rail, and it just made me sick. What kind of God would abuse his own son that way? I would never do such a thing to my children. Why should I even want that kind of God to love me?"

Sandra nodded, thankful that she had studied about atonement theory and the negative responses some people had to some of the theories. She realized that Nicole was having a genuine spiritual crisis, and that she needed to address those questions first, and leave discussion of the affair with Ed—though it was not unrelated—until later. She took a sip of coffee and tried to decide where to begin.

XIII.

The Trinity at Trinity Church

K ate and Mark were new members at Trinity Church. Like many of their friends, they had drifted out of church during their college years, but now, in their late twenties and expecting their first child, they felt it was time to reclaim their religious heritage and find a church home where they could raise their children in the Christian faith.

They had also believed that joining a church would help them make friends and establish themselves in the city where they had moved when Mark was offered a job with a prestigious law firm. One of the senior partners had actually mentioned "a church" in the list of organizations that Mark would be expected to affiliate himself with; others on the list included the local chapter of the alumni association of the state university (from which Mark and Kate had both graduated) and either the Rotary or Kiwanis clubs—Mark was allowed to choose which of the club meetings he would attend each week, as partners were available to sponsor him in either one.

Although he didn't say so to his colleague, Mark was uncomfortable with the idea of deliberately using a church in order to form relationships with potential clients. He and Kate had both been quite involved with the youth groups in their small hometown churches, and he had always assumed that a church would play a role in their lives once they had settled down. Partly just to prove to himself that he was taking the religion part of his church-going seriously, he had insisted that they visit a number of churches before they settled on Trinity.

They liked Trinity because it had a good nursery and an active program for preschoolers, but also because there was a fairly large number of twenty- and-thirty-somethings who were serious about Bible study, mission projects, and the like. The worship services were well-planned and usually meaningful, and the ministerial staff was vigorous and actively fostered theological reflection among the laity.

Kate had taken several women's studies courses in college, and she was particularly pleased at the use of inclusive language in the congregation's services and other gatherings. Although Mark didn't share his wife's enthusiasm for inclusive language, he also didn't have any problem with the church's use of it—or at least, he had no problems until a Sunday morning about three months after they joined the congregation, and about two months before their own baby was expected to arrive.

One of the other couples in their Bible study class had invited about a dozen people to their home for a cookout after worship that day, and so there were several long-time members present when Mark pulled that morning's bulletin out of his pocket and said, "What's going on with the baptism services here? That child who got baptized this morning had different words said over her than I've ever heard before. Listen to this!" Then he read aloud from the bulletin insert the part of the ritual where the pastor had put water on the baby's head and said, "Elizabeth Ann, I baptize you in the name of God the Mother and Father of us all, and in the name of God's Son Jesus Christ, and in the name of God's Holy Spirit."

"So, what's wrong with that?" Kate asked.

"Well, not being a lawyer, you may not realize how significant language is," he began. "In a contract, or a covenant, how you put the words together matters."

"Excuse me?" Kate replied. "I don't realize that language matters? Which one of us majored in English and which one said he was going to do something important with his life?"

"Um, I sense that maybe I didn't put that just right," Mark said.

"You think?" Kate responded.

One of the hosts, Sally, was standing nearby and intervened. "Tempting as it is to watch you hang yourself," she told Mark— "and as an English major myself, I have to say I am truly tempted—I probably ought to mention that I was on the Worship Committee when we made the change in the ritual. Maybe I can answer some of your questions about how we decided to do that."

Sally found herself talking not just to Mark and Kate, but to several other couples who had stopped their own conversations to listen. She explained that it was the practice of the senior pastor at Trinity to meet with the parents of children to be baptized, as well as with any adult candidates for baptism, to go over the baptismal service and to talk about what baptism meant. In one such conversation a few years ago, someone had remarked that in the context of the inclusive God-language normally used in worship at Trinity, the baptismal formula with its emphatic "masculinity" had come to sound increasingly odd. Others had agreed, saying that the formula seemed somehow to misrepresent the God they worshiped and were taught about at Trinity. They wondered whether some alternative formulation couldn't be used. The pastor had been very receptive to their concerns. Sally didn't recall just what was done about the formula for that particular occasion, but she did remember that it was that conversation that had led the ministerial staff to bring the issue to the Worship Committee, along with the proposed new wording. After discussion, the new formulation was approved by the Worship Committee and then by the Administrative Council, but with the understanding that candidates or parents would be free to opt for the traditional formula if they preferred it.

"So, it was a male versus female kind of thing," Mark said.

Before Sally could respond, her husband, Philip, who had also stopped to listen, broke in. "That's not true at all," he insisted. "There are lots of men at Trinity who are just as committed to the newer language for all sorts of reasons. And if I remember correctly, some of the people who were most hesitant about the change at first were women."

"That's right," Sally agreed. "Now that we've gotten accustomed to it, this arrangement has been satisfactory to everybody, I think, for the past few years. But if you and Kate want the traditional language for your baby's baptism, the pastor will be happy to use it, I know."

"Well, I don't think there's any necessity to have just Father language for our baby," Kate said, at just the same time as Mark responded, "Good. But our baby's not the only one I'm worried about. I'm wondering whether that baby baptized this morning even received a Christian baptism."

Another member of the group spoke up. "Maybe Mark's right," she said. "I mean, when we studied Matthew's Gospel, didn't we read about Jesus telling his followers to baptize 'in the name of the Father and of the Son and of the Holy Spirit'? Are people really baptized if those words aren't used? And would Trinity's baptisms be recognized by other churches?"

"Of course they would," one person responded. But another said, "I don't know. Maybe we ought to check into these things."

"I guess it's time the Worship Committee re-examined the issue," Sally said. "We had good reasons for doing what we did, but if there are questions about whether we're really practicing Christian baptism, then we need to answer those questions. Mark, we have a committee meeting scheduled in a couple of weeks. Will you come and express your concerns to us?"

Mark nodded, and Kate said, "I think I'd better plan to come, too."

The next day, Sally invited the senior pastor, Rosemarie, to lunch. Over shrimp salads, Sally told her that Mark and Kate would be coming to the next Worship Committee meeting with their divergent opinions about their baby's baptism. "And it's more than that," she said. "Mark is questioning whether babies like Elizabeth would be recognized as baptized by other congregations. Tell me, are the words really that important?"

XIV.

God's Will or God's Won't

Bob's first Monday at St. Miscellaneous was complicated by the fact that his predecessor had scheduled Vacation Bible School for that week. Although Bob and his family were busy moving into the parsonage, he had agreed to give a devotional each morning during the opening exercises.

He wanted to use the gathering to try to get to know some of the adult volunteers, as well, and he had asked Marie, the Staff-Parish Relations chair, to stay close to him and introduce him to people. One of the persons he met was Angela. Angela stood out in the crowd for several reasons. Unlike the other adults, who were dressed in casual clothes appropriate for working with young children who'd be eating and doing crafts, she was dressed in a suit. She wore high heels and what seemed to Bob to be a great deal of costume jewelry. Her hair was heavily sprayed into the kind of style that his wife called "helmet hair," and as he looked at Angela's face, he was immediately struck by the amount of makeup she wore—too much for any occasion, much less VBS, he thought. She had obviously taken great care in dressing that morning, and yet her attire was almost ridiculous in that setting.

Aside from her physical appearance, there was something out of place about her manner, too. Her voice and movements betrayed something—a brittleness, he thought—that seemed wrong for the playful setting of VBS. But three or four sentences into his conversation with her, he discovered a reason for that. "My son Stephen drowned two weeks ago," she said. "That's why I'm here. I know that I have to get right with God now."

Bob was able to say only, "I'm so sorry this has happened," before a bell rang. Angela said that she had to go help with the class to which she'd been assigned, and she hurried away. He turned to Marie, and his expression must have conveyed his bewilderment, because she began to explain about Angela's presence before he said a word. She told him that Angela had been a member of that church many years ago before she had left the state, and that while she had moved back to the community about a year earlier, she had not returned to church until after Stephen died.

She said that Angela; her four-year-old son, Stephen; her six-year-old daughter, Melissa; and her boyfriend, Mark, who lived with them, had gone two Sunday mornings previously to a popular spot for cookouts on the banks of a scenic river about forty-five miles away. The children were playing and wading in the shallows near the river's edge while Angela sat nearby. About 11:30, when she began setting out their lunch, Angela discovered she had forgotten some item and returned to their truck, parked some distance away, to get it, leaving the children in the water. When she returned, people were screaming, and her son was missing, having been dragged by the current into the river. He had been pulled under the water almost immediately, and since he could not swim, it was clear that he had drowned. Sure enough, his body was recovered a few hours later at a spot downriver where bodies of drowning victims had emerged before.

"It was a tragedy," Marie said, "but at least they found the body and she didn't have to deal with false hope. And somebody else will tell you, so I might as well go ahead and do it—Angela has a drinking problem, and she was probably at least half drunk when it happened. Why else would a mother go off and leave a four-year-old wading in a river? And she says she didn't know it was dangerous, but the river was swollen from all the rains we've had, and the current was swifter than ever. She went on television the next day, she says 'to warn other people' that the river is dangerous for children. But what kind of person doesn't know that already?"

Marie was correct about at least one thing, Bob found. Other people were indeed eager to tell him about the event. By that evening, he had learned that the assumption of blame for Angela which underlay Marie's narrative was common, with those who spoke of the accident as alcohol-related being more forthcoming about their opinion than those who left the story at implied gross negligence and stupidity on Angela's part.

He also learned that Stephen's funeral had been conducted at a funeral home by Samuel Jennings, a United Methodist pastor who lived in the community near where the drowning had occurred. He had been summoned to the scene by bystanders. Jennings had stayed with the family until the body was found, accompanied them to the funeral home, and some thought he had probably even paid for the funeral himself, since Angela and her boyfriend had almost no financial resources and an anonymous donor had stepped forward to cover the expenses. Jennings was new to the pastorate, and Bob had not had an opportunity to meet him, but it was clear that he had gone "above and beyond the call" with Angela, who was not even Jennings' parishioner or likely to become so, since she lived so far away.

That evening, Bob talked about Angela with his wife, Hannah, whose professional background had given her some insight into issues surrounding death and dying. He told her how strange Angela's presence had seemed to him at VBS that morning. "Well, I have to give her credit," Hannah responded, "that she was up and dressed. If one of our kids died, I wouldn't get out of bed for a year. And I certainly wouldn't go someplace where there were lots of healthy children two weeks later." Regarding the reactions of the other parishioners, Hannah said, their tendency to blame Angela was not as surprising as Bob might think. "Losing a child is the ultimate tragedy," she said, "and no one wants to think it could happen to them. We'd all rather pretend it never happened, and when we can't do that, we look for some way the parent was at fault, because it separates them from good, careful parents like us, and we can maintain the fantasy that we're immune from that kind of thing. Besides," she added, "it's really hard to make a case for her not being at fault. Who does leave a four-year-old who can't swim wading in a river? I wonder how she'll be able to deal with the guilt. It's the kind of thing that could easily destroy a parent, I would think."

"Everything you said makes sense," Bob admitted, "but there's still something way off kilter about all this." He resolved to make an opportunity the next day to talk with Angela at greater length.

On Tuesday, while the class she was helping with was busy with the music instructor, he asked her into his office for a talk. He let Angela tell the story of what had happened, which she clearly needed to do, and then, without his prompting, she turned to her presence at VBS. "Reverend Jennings told me I have to get back in church," she said. "It happened at just the time on Sunday morning that we should have been in church. I should have been here instead of out on the river. But he explained to me that it was God's will that Stephen died. I understand that now."

"God's will?" Bob echoed. "Doesn't that make you awfully angry at God?"

"Oh, no," Angela answered quickly. "Reverend Jennings explained that I absolutely can't be angry at God about this. That would be wrong. He told me that something much worse would probably have happened to Stephen later in his life, and that God was sparing him from that by taking him now."

She went on to elaborate about how kind Reverend Jennings had been and to restate several times, in various ways, all that he had said about God's taking Stephen's life and how she had to get her own life right with God now. As she talked, Bob wondered how to respond to what she was saying.

XV.

Su Casa, Mi Casa

I an and Abigail had been co-pastors at Elm Street Church, an urban congregation with about two hundred in worship each Sunday morning, for about three months. The congregation was the most problematic place of service that either of them had ever experienced. One reason for their difficulties—though by no means the only one—was the nature of the congregation's continuing attachment with Bradley, the former minister. The Elm Street congregation had been established five years previously through the merger of two other congregations, and Bradley had served as its founding pastor.

The long list of severely troubled parishioners they were encountering included Roberta, a woman whom Abigail judged to be in her late thirties, or just a few years younger than she and Ian were. Roberta was about three years into a second marriage; it was also a second marriage for her husband, Hank. There were no children from any of these unions.

Roberta and Hank had met at Elm Street Church. The former pastor, Bradley, had performed their wedding. The congregation had a strong emotional investment in the couple, even though Hank had stopped attending worship soon after the wedding. Roberta continued to attend faithfully, adding her beautiful, solo-quality voice to the choir most Sunday mornings and participating in a smaller choral group that performed at Elm Street and in other venues around the city, enhancing the reputation of the church in the area.

Roberta had come to Ian soon after the co-pastors' arrival for counseling about problems in her marriage. Although she seemed very upset, she was not able to articulate what was bothering her very well, and he had tried to refer her to a therapist. Although she held a teaching job that had good health benefits, she insisted that she couldn't put therapy on her insurance for fear she'd be fired and that she didn't have the money to pay for it herself. She ignored the information that both he and Abigail offered about free sources of help.

Several parishioners had already spoken to Abigail about their fears that Roberta was being battered by Hank. She certainly exhibited some of the signs, including frequent bruises for which she gave unconvincing explanations whenever anyone questioned her. When she came in one day to discuss her marital problems with Abigail, the pastor asked her point blank whether she was battered. Roberta denied it. In the next breath, she explained that Hank was out of work and therefore under extreme stress. She insisted, however, that although her first husband had abused her, Hank had never hit her. Neither Ian nor Abigail believed these assurances to be true.

Even though Ian and Abigail told Roberta on several occasions that they were not trained as therapists and that Roberta should definitely follow up on the counseling referrals they had provided, she did not do so. She kept begging them for appointments instead. On one such occasion, Abigail had acquiesced and made an appointment at an inconvenient time for herself. Then, Roberta simply failed to show up for the session. When Abigail called her three days later, Roberta did not mention the missed appointment until Abigail questioned her, and then just said that she had been "busy" that day and "couldn't call."

By that time, though, Abigail had come to expect that kind of behavior. Roberta had frequently demonstrated her unreliability. For instance, she had agreed five weeks ahead of time to do a program on a topic in the area of education for a women's group that Abigail led. Roberta then called Abigail just an hour before the meeting to say that she just didn't feel like coming. When Abigail explained to the group that Roberta had cancelled at the last minute, and that she had had to improvise a program for them, they actually laughed at Abigail for thinking that Roberta would show up.

In another instance, Roberta came to the early service one Sunday morning to perform with the choral group, which was scheduled to perform at the later service as well. About fifteen minutes before the second service was to start, she decided she was too upset about her marriage to sing, and when she came to Abigail's office to say she was going home, she broke down into tears. Abigail explained she had to leave to begin the eleven o'clock worship service, at which she was scheduled to preach; Roberta kept on talking and crying. Abigail offered to send someone else in to stay with her during worship; Roberta said she only wanted Abigail. Abigail tried to make an agreement to see her after worship or any other time that day; Roberta said she wanted to go home and sleep, and wouldn't want to come back later, and that she wanted to talk right then. Abigail finally left Roberta alone in the office, and entered the sanctuary a few minutes late for worship.

In mid-September, Ian and Abigail were scheduled to attend a continuing education event in another state. Both of them were very much looking forward to a few days away, with some time to try to evaluate what was happening at Elm Street Church, and some time to relax, away from the strain that the church's problems had put on their own relationship. They were to leave for the airport quite early on Monday morning, and Sunday evening found them busy with packing and all the last-minute details that needed attending to before they could get away. Around nine o'clock, the telephone rang. Abigail answered and heard Roberta's voice on the line.

"I know you're going to be out of town this week," she said. "Can I stay at your house while you're gone? Hank and I are having problems, and we just need some 'cooling off' time. I can't afford to go anywhere else. And Bradley and Monica always let me stay there."

Within seconds, a list of reasons this was not a good idea flashed through Abigail's mind. Her personal papers included not only records from her previous job as a consultant, some of which contained sensitive information about her clients' businesses, but also process papers from her seminary internship, including "verbatims" of conversations with parishioners and assessments of how she had handled problems that occurred at that church. There were also documents at the house that the previous pastor at Elm Street had compiled relating to a possible case of sexual misconduct on the part of a former staff member. Abigail kept all this material at home rather than in her church office precisely so that no one other than she and Ian would ever have access to them. The house was protected by a burglar alarm system, but Roberta would have to have the code if she stayed there.

Besides, even if she and Ian could arrange to get every sensitive piece of paper under lock and key before the next morning, Abigail just didn't want Roberta there. Abigail was an only child and had always been used to having privacy at home. Her level of trust in Roberta did not even approach the level of trust she would need to be comfortable about leaving someone in her home. The mere thought of Roberta being free to poke around in her things was offensive.

However, none of these reasons seemed like something she could put into words to Roberta, who was waiting on the line for an answer. Further, she knew that if she refused, it was possible that Hank would seriously injure Roberta while they were gone. The seconds were ticking past, and her hesitation already seemed uncomfortably long; she knew she had to say something.

XVI.

Things That Go Bump in the Night

Nine-year-old Ginny was one of Abigail's favorite parishioners. Ginny was an only child who was with adults more than with other children and who was unusually serious for her years.

Her mother, Sharon, had been active in church as a child and as a youth, and she saw that Ginny was at every church function available to children. In fact, she even brought her along to some adult events where Ginny was the only child in attendance. Ginny's dad had been unemployed or underemployed for years and the family was not secure financially, but Ginny was well cared for. Sharon saw to it that Ginny was always perfectly groomed and that she always had suitable clothing—usually dresses—to wear to church activities. Ginny's long blond hair was always clean and shining, and she looked in some respects like Alice in Wonderland, though in slightly less structured attire.

Abigail was not the only adult who had a special fondness for Ginny. Another was Cecilia, who had served as Sunday school superintendent at Elm Street Church before she contracted terminal cancer. Cecilia was liked and respected by the entire church. She had also sung in the choir, been active in the women's society, and served in several other key lay leadership posts before her illness. Still, it was through Sunday school that Ginny had known her best.

Because Cecilia was still young, in her late thirties, and because she was the daughter of prominent and well-liked older members, the congregation viewed her illness and impending death as particularly tragic.

The church had rallied around her in her illness, and members visited her at her parents' home frequently, not forgetting her as she grew less and less able to participate in church activities. As her cancer progressed, she lost the ability to walk and to care for herself, and finally, even the ability to speak. Sharon took Ginny to visit frequently, so Ginny had seen Cecilia's decline for herself.

When Cecilia's death finally came, the funeral was scheduled for a school day. Ginny expressed a desire to come, and Sharon asked Abigail whether she should bring her. Abigail counseled that she should be allowed to come, and Sharon brought her. The funeral was a good one, with a large crowd in attendance, uplifting music, and a focus on celebrating the positive contributions of Cecilia's life, along with mourning her death. Ginny did not seem to be inappropriately upset by the ritual, nor inappropriately uninvolved. She cried, as did many, many others. Ginny was not present for the burial itself.

Before worship two weeks later, Sharon asked to speak with Abigail, and told her that Ginny had seen Cecilia's ghost the night before. "She's pretty shaken up," Sharon said. "We were coming home from the store in the van, and she was in the back seat. The van's television was turned off, but the screen is still kind of reflective, and Ginny saw Cecilia's face on the screen. She screamed. It scared me half to death. She didn't sleep much last night—I had to let her sleep in our bed—and I couldn't get her up for church this morning. Would you be willing to talk to her about this?"

After explaining that she was not a trained counselor and that Ginny might need to see such a person, as well, Abigail agreed to see Ginny that afternoon to talk about what had happened from a Christian perspective. At the appointed hour, Sharon arrived at the church with Ginny. "I'm going to let you talk while I run an errand," Sharon told them. After suggesting that Sharon return in about an hour, Abigail took Ginny into her office where they got comfortable on the couch.

Ginny was even quieter than usual, and Abigail saw that it would be up to her to start the conversation.

XVII.

Intercultural Retreat

Among Bob's more enjoyable tasks during his first four years at St. Miscellaneous United Methodist Church was his service on the Board of Directors at the nearby state university's campus ministry. Among the local church representatives on the board, he was the most active participant in the programming. Part of the reward for his involvement was his deepening friendship with the campus minister, Andy.

When Bob joined the board, Andy asked if he would help with the Intercultural Retreat held each year in the fall. This retreat was a fairly new program at that time, having been created some three years previously by Andy and several international students. Twenty new international students, twenty returning international students, and twenty students from the United States spent a weekend together in a camp setting, learning about one another's customs and faiths, and hearing from experts and from one another about what it is like to live in a different country and then to return to one's own home. The retreat took a good bit of planning, if for no other reason than because the dietary restrictions of the Hindu and Muslim students, along with those who were vegetarians, made it a challenge to plan three days' worth of meals that everyone could enjoy.

Andy had formed good relationships with many of the university staff, and he was able to get funding assistance from the International Student Office and even some from the Student Government Association to help cover the expenses for the retreat, which always included the cost of bringing in a speaker well-informed about intercultural experiences.

Bob's particular assignment that first year was to facilitate one of the small groups that met from time to time throughout the weekend to discuss and compare the students' religious backgrounds and value systems. Although persons from the different faith traditions—Christian, Buddhist, Jewish, Hindu, Muslim, and so on—were asked to take turns giving a blessing for the food at mealtimes, there was no formal worship as such at the retreat, since the spectrum of faiths represented was so broad. In Bob's view, the most religious aspect of the gathering was the remarkably honest and thoughtful sharing that went on in the small group settings.

Although he was not sure what to expect, Bob found that that first retreat was one of the most interesting and rewarding weekends he had spent in ministry. He was careful to block out that weekend the next three autumns so that he could be present, and he continued to find it a most fruitful activity, not just for the students but also for him and the other leaders.

As was pretty much inevitable, the time came when Andy was offered a different position and accepted it, and Bob had to bid his friend good-bye. Clarence, the minister who was appointed to take Andy's place, held significantly different theological views, and as Bob expected, he made a number of changes in how the ministry was conducted. Some of these Bob could approve, while others he felt he just had to accept.

Then, at a late August board meeting, Clarence announced in a fairly dismissive way that the upcoming Intercultural Retreat was being cancelled. Bob was dismayed and asked for a fuller explanation. Clarence said that in his meetings with representatives from the International Student Office and the Student Government Association, he had told them that he intended to have Christian worship as part of the activities each day at the retreat. After extensive discussion, the two organizations had decided that if Clarence would not agree to have inter-faith services or no worship services at all, they would have to withdraw their funding.

"I told them I wasn't about to spend ministry money and my own time on a gathering that wasn't Christian in its focus," Clarence said. "There's no point taking those other students out there if they don't have an opportunity to give their hearts to the Lord."

Several of the long-time board members were quite upset that Clarence had made the decision single-handedly and also disagreed with his reasoning. A couple of brand new members whom Clarence had recruited were, on the other hand, quite supportive of his decision and were pleased that he wanted to direct the ministry's resources toward the conversion of students who practiced other faiths.

Bob began to speak about his experiences on the retreats, and commented that Andy had always said that the international students were the very ones we needed to be in conversation with, because they were usually among the most intelligent and often the most affluent citizens of their countries and could therefore be expected to assume leadership roles there after they returned home. "All the more reason to convert them now, while we have a chance," one new board member retorted.

Several people began to speak at once, some angrily, and the board president called for a ten-minute break to give people time to gather their thoughts and their tempers. Bob found several long-time members gathering around him and trying to form a strategy to keep the retreat from being cancelled. "You shouldn't have mentioned Andy," one of them said. "That's just guaranteed to make Clarence feel like he's being compared unfavorably, and it's important for us to support him where we can. But this is just too big a change, and too much of a switch in our emphasis." Another one spoke up, "It's not just that it's a change, or that Clarence made it without appropriate consultation. I think it's just wrong for us to insist that a student who's faithfully practicing another faith even needs to convert to Christianity." After more discussion, they agreed that if Clarence were going to insist on having worship services where students were actively pressured to accept Christ, it probably would be better to cancel. Yet none of them wanted to give up sponsoring the retreat as it had been held in the past.

They decided that Bob, who had been the most deeply involved with the previous retreats, should be the one to "speak for our side," as one woman put it, and when the meeting resumed, make the case for continuing the retreat with the same emphasis as before.

XVIII.

Sleepover

Larry, the minister at a church in Mediumville, was single and thirty-seven at the time of his appointment there. He had been engaged a few years before, but things fell apart right before the wedding, and he hadn't found anyone else he felt quite the same way about since that time. He sometimes found being single a bit of a problem in ministry, because some churches still seemed to expect him to come as a "package deal"—with a wife who would teach Sunday school and play the piano—and because the hierarchy in his denomination appeared hesitant to let single men pastor larger churches. One friend of his actually suggested that Larry and a single female pastor whom they knew to be a "closeted" lesbian should get married and then divorce, because divorced pastors seemed to do better in their conference than never-married ones. Larry laughed it off as the joke that it was, but the underlying truth that made it funny—that such a sham marriage might actually be a help to his career—lingered in his mind and retained the power to hurt him when he thought of it.

Mediumville was a suburb of a large city, but one that was fairly self-contained and that still had a small town feel to it. The church's parsonage had clearly been chosen with a "typical" minister's family in mind: three bedrooms, two baths, a fenced backyard, and a double carport would have provided plenty of space for the wife and children Larry didn't have. Still, Larry had become accustomed to being single, and he did not usually see the house as calling attention to what he lacked, but rather as giving him plenty of room to spread out in, his dog a nice big yard to play in, and his friends a place to stay when they came to the city.

One such friend was Tim, whom Larry had known since college. They had both been active participants in the campus ministry organization and in other groups interested in peace and justice. While Tim was homosexual and Larry was heterosexual, both thought it wrong to discriminate against anyone on the basis of sexual orientation. Nevertheless, their college activism had focused on other issues, such as racism.

After college, both Larry and Tim had started seminary, but because their denomination was not open to gay or lesbian ministers (a position that Larry hoped would change in the coming years), Tim had left seminary and pursued a master's degree in social work instead. He now had a job in a neighboring state with a community action agency that aided the poor. He still had a deep interest in theology, however, and he and Larry had kept in touch through the years, visiting with each other occasionally and talking about theology when either chanced to be visiting the other's city.

About two months after Larry's appointment at Mediumville, Tim was assigned to take a course taught at a university in the city adjoining Mediumville. The course would give him expertise in an area of social work his agency wished to add to their portfolio of services. It was a graduate-level course, but because most students were working professionals, it was designed so that much of the work could be accomplished over the Internet. The students were to meet six times during the course of the semester, spending all day Friday and then Saturday morning in class. Because of the distance from the city where he worked, Tim planned to drive in on Thursday evening; he would naturally also stay in the city Friday night and then drive home on Saturday afternoon.

When Tim phoned to tell Larry that he'd be in the city for the course, it seemed only natural to Larry to offer him a guest room in the parsonage. They had stayed at each other's homes in the past. Further, Larry knew that the agency Tim worked for operated on a shoestring budget, and that Tim's salary was not huge. Whether Tim or the agency had to pay for a hotel room, it would be a strain, as Larry knew without even discussing the matter. He offered, and Tim accepted the hospitality gratefully.

Over the first eight weeks of the semester, Tim stayed with Larry three times. Each time, Tim treated Larry to a nice dinner out in the city, and once, they dined with a clergy couple, Abigail and Ian, who were appointed in the adjoining city and whom Tim also knew from seminary. Because Tim was tired from the driving and studying on top of his job, and from concentrating in a classroom all day, which was something he hadn't done in a number of years, they usually returned to the parsonage fairly early. Both of them enjoyed having time to talk together, to catch up on what was happening in their lives, and to discuss matters relating to the church, which Tim still cared about deeply, although he had moved to a denomination that was more actively welcoming to gay and lesbian people.

In the middle of the week after Tim's third visit, Larry received a call from the chair of his Staff-Parish Relations Committee. The chairperson, who seemed embarrassed and somewhat annoyed, said that there would be a meeting of the committee the following evening, and that Larry should plan to attend. He said that every member of the committee had received a call "about the problem," and he felt he had no choice but to call the meeting. When Larry asked what problem the chairperson meant, he said that he did not want to get into details over the phone, but he did tell Larry that the complaints centered around the fact that a man was staying overnight at the parsonage, and it just looked "funny" for a single man to have another man spending the night with him. At first, he did not want to tell Larry who had made the complaints, but since so many people had been contacted, he decided that Larry would no doubt find out anyway, and told him the source.

He said that the members had all received calls from a retired couple who belonged to the church and who lived on the same street as the parsonage. They had been particular friends with the former pastor's wife, and she had joined them for coffee and watched a favorite soap opera with them several times a week. Larry had visited with the couple one evening, saw them at church on Sundays, and waved if they were outside as he passed their house, but since he worked at the office almost every weekday, he did not have the opportunity to form the kind of relationship they had enjoyed with the previous parsonage inhabitant, and in truth, he would have lacked the desire to do so had the opportunity been present.

"Some of the other committee members are more upset about it than I am," the chairperson said, "and it would really be better if we just talked about it tomorrow night." He hung up as soon as he could, leaving Larry to deal with a wide range of emotions, not the least of which was anger.

As he often did when he was faced with a problem, Larry called his friends Abigail and Ian, and wound up at their parsonage discussing the issue. After he had vented some of his fury about being "spied on" by his members, he was able to begin to think about the questions the committee might ask, the objections they might have, and how he might best be able to respond to them.

"I don't think they could possibly *know* that Tim is gay," he said. "Unless they traced his license plate number—which at this point I'm not ready to rule out—they don't even know who he is, much less anything about him. But what if they ask me if he's gay? What if they ask me if I'm gay? I don't think being gay ought to keep people from being ordained. If I make a big deal of insisting that I'm not gay, am I selling out my beliefs that it ought not to matter?"

"Good grief," Abigail said. "I'm not ready to answer that yet; I'm having a hard time dealing with the fact that this is even happening. And I'm trying to see it from your committee's point of view. The only experience I have to draw on—the only thing that's ever happened to me that even vaguely relates to this—is that once when I attended a church-sponsored national convention, we had roommates assigned to us, and mine was a woman who was a lesbian. It made me feel a little weird, I have to tell you. There are guys who are my friends that I could have stayed in a room with if I had needed to, but I certainly wouldn't share a room with a man who was a stranger; and sharing one with her, when she was a complete stranger, felt a little bit like that to me. If I were a single pastor, I can see why my congregation wouldn't want me to have a single guy spend the night in the parsonage. But if it were a woman staying with me, I don't think they'd think twice about it. Two women staying together are assumed to be friends; two men staying together are much likelier to be assumed to be gay. It's weird how our culture regards things."

"Are you saying I shouldn't have Tim there since he's gay?" Larry asked her.

"No," she denied quickly, "I'm not saying that at all. I'm saying—well, I don't know what I'm saying. This is a truly confusing situation you're in. But what's not confusing is that Tim is your friend and that's why you let him stay there and that sex had nothing to do with it. But unfortunately, your SPR committee may not see it that way."

"Well, obviously they don't," Ian put in. "Just by calling the meeting, they're asking about your sexual orientation. And I understand why you have ethical qualms about insisting you're not gay, but since you're not, and since we don't ordain openly gay men, then it might not make sense to refuse to 'admit' you're straight."

"Well, I get what you mean," said Larry, "though I'm not sure yet whether I agree with it. But what about Tim? Should I tell them he's gay if they ask? Do I even have the right to talk about his sexual orientation with them? And if I refuse to answer, isn't that like saying that he's gay? And where is all this heading? If I decide he shouldn't stay there just for appearance's sake, what will I tell him? 'You can't spend the night in my parsonage because you're gay'? That would be saying there's something immoral about who he is—that he could stay there if he were a 'moral' person. And it feels to me that it's saying there's something wrong with me, too. You two could have anybody stay here that you wanted—and I can't because I'm single? What's the matter with this church, anyway?"

Ian and Abigail looked at each other, each hoping the other would be inspired with the right thing to say.

XIX.

Die or Dialysis

Bob, the pastor at St. Miscellaneous, was always attentive to the needs of the ill and the shut-ins in his congregation. Thus, he had formed a good relationship with Olive, an elderly woman who had been able to attend worship only rarely during his five years at the church.

Olive was afflicted with a number of illnesses, including diabetes and various kinds of heart trouble. She was a breast cancer survivor, and he knew that she was frequently concerned that that disease might return. However, her most serious health problem, or at least the ailment that offered the most immediate chance of fatality for her, was kidney failure. Ever since Bob had been at St. Misc, Olive had been on dialysis, a method of "cleaning" a patient's blood when the kidneys are no longer able to function adequately. It involved hooking her to a machine that took her blood out, artificially removed waste and excess fluid, and returned the blood to her body. Bob knew that she had been on dialysis for at least a couple of years before he came to St. Misc, but she had to undergo what was for her a long and exhausting procedure more frequently nowadays than she had in the past in order to survive.

At eighty-five, Olive was still mentally acute, and she and Bob had engaged in many discussions about the Christian faith over the past five years. He knew that she read the Bible and had private devotions every day. In the past few months, he had watched her decline in spirits, and she mentioned far more frequently how tired she constantly felt. Because of her declining health, it seemed to him, and to her, that she spent as much time in the hospital as she did in the nursing home, which she had had to move into about two years before.

In mid-November, Bob visited Olive to take her the Eucharist. He found her in tears, alone in her room in the nursing home. When he inquired what was wrong, Olive said that she was crying "because I'm just so tired. I just don't want to have dialysis anymore. I've lived a long life, and I don't think I ought to have to suffer with it any longer." She explained that she was thinking of asking her doctors to discontinue the dialysis after the first of the year, after she had spent one more holiday season with her grown children and grandchildren.

"Would it be a sin if I stopped having dialysis?" she asked tearfully.

Bob responded that in her situation, he didn't think it would be sinful to stop the procedure, but that he wasn't necessarily convinced it was the proper course for her to take. "Maybe I'm being selfish, but I would miss you," he said. "And it's something your children and grandchildren need to be consulted about, as well," he said. After further conversation, during which he urged Olive not to make any firm decision just yet, and a time of prayer together, Bob left with a promise to visit her again in a few days.

Before that could happen, he received a call from Olive's oldest daughter, Maxine. Maxine and her sister belonged to a generation of white Protestants who had strong Roman Catholic leanings because their parents had put them in Roman Catholic schools when the public schools were desegregated in the 1960s; they remained there until the Catholic school system in that area was integrated a few years later. In this way, several years' worth of instruction from priests and nuns became a significant part of the spiritual formation of many white Protestant children in the area, and the notion that suicide was such a sinful act that it would even preclude one's burial in consecrated ground was thus a part of Maxine's and her sister's religious understanding.

She was therefore very upset with Bob for having told her mother that it would not be sinful for her to discontinue dialysis. "How can you call yourself a minister?" she demanded. "You're telling my mother it's OK to kill herself. I don't want her to die, and if you were really a man of God, you'd explain to her that it's up to God, not you or her, to decide when it's her time."

Bob expressed his sorrow for her pain, and asked if she would come by his office that afternoon so that they could discuss things face-to-face. She agreed. As he completed his tasks for the morning, he thought about the encounter to come and dreaded it. He knew that along with coping with Maxine's grief, he would need to present a coherent explanation to Maxine as to why he believed that her mother would not be following a sinful course if indeed she should decide to discontinue the life-saving procedure.

X X .

Home, Sweet Home

Miranda had been the minister at an ecumenically funded campus ministry at a state university for seven years. One of the activities was a Wednesday night discussion group that followed a short, informal worship built around a devotional or homily. About thirty students were attending it that semester.

Campus ministry suited Miranda almost perfectly, and she was happier than she had been serving in the local congregation. For one thing, she was convinced that college students who were active in a religious community were shaped spiritually by that experience throughout the rest of their lives, and that made the work especially meaningful to her.

Although she would have liked to spend the holidays with her parents and siblings, who lived several hours away from the campus where she served, she believed that the Thanksgiving and Holy Week breaks provided such a perfect opportunity for students to experience a mission trip that she always organized a journey for them at those times. To Miranda, working in a completely different culture seemed a crucial piece of the learning experience, and so despite the additional problems involved, she chose locations in Mexico or Central America for the trips.

This year, though, she had received a request for her students to come and help with repairs on a building being used by a Hispanic congregation called Nueva Esperanza. The building, located in another part of the state, had formerly been owned by an Anglo group who had let it deteriorate over the years as the congregation aged. There was much work that had to be accomplished to make the building suitable again for a younger congregation whose children needed facilities for Sunday school and youth activities.

Miranda had found her planning to be much simpler for a domestic trip, and she was as satisfied with the intercultural exposure her students received as if they had gone to another country. In fact, she thought that letting the students realize how disparate experiences could be in the United States for people whose skin was a different color from theirs or who spoke a different language was perhaps even more valuable than reinforcing their knowledge that life—and religious practices—would be quite different in a foreign land.

Nueva Esperanza had been the recipient of construction assistance from several congregations before the campus ministry group arrived, and they had developed a schedule for bringing the visitors and the members of the congregation into contact with one another. Some of the women had opened a Mexican restaurant, and they brought food for Miranda and the fourteen students each day when they paused from their work for a lunch break. After work ceased late each afternoon, a member of the congregation told his or her story to the students within the context of an evening devotional led by the pastor.

Because Thursday was Thanksgiving Day, the students ate a noon meal with the pastor and his family, and afterward, he spoke to them about Hebrews 13:2. He reminded them that the verse, which urges that Christians never neglect to show hospitality to strangers, states that those who do welcome strangers may be entertaining angels unaware. "You are angels to us," he told the students, "but we are not unaware of it. You are angels to our children, who need a safe, clean place to learn about our Lord."

On Friday, the group heard from Antonio, a Mexican who had lived in this country for almost ten years. He came straight from his job to the gathering, and he was still dressed in the grimy garments he wore to work on a chicken farm. Though such labor was hard and unpleasant, he did not complain. Instead, he talked to the group about how grateful he was to be in this country. In fact, he had made his way over the border twice, after being discovered and sent back the first time. The large amount he had paid a coyote to smuggle him across was, of course, not refunded.

Antonio talked about how he had worked and saved to get enough money to bring his wife and children to the United States. Though neither he nor his wife was in the country legally, they both had jobs that they had obtained using fake Social Security numbers. The companies for which they worked deducted state and federal income tax and Social Security taxes from their paychecks, but they could not file for refunds and could never collect retirement from the government because the Social Security numbers were not really valid. Thus, when he heard people talk about illegal aliens who don't pay taxes, he was hurt by the unfairness of the claim.

He talked about how his children had not had enough to eat and lacked medical care in Mexico, and how thankful they were that their parents had managed to find better lives in this country. Antonio had quit school himself at age twelve to go to work to earn 90 pesos a week. His $7.25 an hour at the chicken farm was more than he had ever dreamed of earning in the Mexican village where he was raised.

Though being separated from one another during the years it had taken him to earn enough money to bring his family to the United States had been hard, the hope that they had of a better life here had let them endure it. Antonio talked proudly about how well his children spoke English, and said that they were all good students, and that his daughter, who had always loved music, was playing an instrument in the school band. Antonio was almost in tears as he spoke of how meaningful their Thanksgiving meal the day before had been to his family. As the light ebbed from the room, Antonio spoke of the children's dangerous journey through the Southwestern desert, and Miranda knew that several of the students were using the growing dark to conceal that they were crying, too.

When the group returned home, Miranda left for a few days with her family, who had grown more or less accustomed to her visits being close to, but never on, Thanksgiving Day. In her absence, the president of the Student Council at the ministry led the Wednesday evening gathering, which focused on the sharing of their experiences by those who made the mission trip with those who had not been able to go.

When Miranda returned to the office on Friday, she found a letter from Nueva Esperanza's pastor. After thanking her and the students again for all the work they did, he wrote, "We're having a service of Los Posadas two weeks from now, and we were hoping some of the students would come back down and play the roles of Mary and Joseph," he said. She was somewhat familiar with the custom, but looked it up to refresh her memory, and discovered that the ritual was a re-enactment of the couple's being turned away from the inn in Bethlehem before finding room in the stable. She was delighted and hopeful that her students could study the ritual as they continued to reflect on their mission trip.

In the early afternoon, two of the students who had been on the trip came by her office. Tom and Cindy were both in their junior year at the university and had been part of the campus ministry organization since they came as first-year students. They asked whether Miranda had time to talk with them, and when she said she did, they settled into chairs in her office.

It was obvious they had something on their minds, and so Miranda let them talk before she brought up the Los Posadas service. "We have something to say that you might not like," Cindy began, "but we talked it through with the whole group Wednesday night when we discussed the mission trip, and we're both pretty sure we know what the right thing to do is."

"The right thing about what?" Miranda asked, thinking that perhaps they wanted to do a fund-raiser of some sort to help the Nueva Esperanza congregation, but unclear as to why they would think she wouldn't like that.

"About Antonio," Tom said. "You know he's in this country illegally."

"Oh. Well, yes, he is," she answered.

"The Bible is really clear about our duty," he said, and he proceeded to quote Romans 13:1-2. Then he added, "We are not supposed to resist the laws, and I'm certain that my Christian duty is to report Antonio to the Immigration Service. He ought to go home. He's breaking the law by being here, and I know about it, so that's what I have to do."

Before he could say more, Cindy broke in, "Anyway, if Tom didn't turn him in, I would—but I think that's the wrong reason. You've taught us that Christians have a responsibility to practice hospitality, like it says in Hebrews, and I think that the laws that keep people out are wrong. We got a lot of Mexico's land dishonestly to begin with, and keeping Mexicans out of 'our' country is so hypocritical of us. Antonio and his family are such sympathetic characters, I just know that if he's arrested, taking the case all the way to the Supreme Court will make everybody see how wrong our policies are. If people just understood what's going on, they would make the legislators do the right thing. It's my duty to try to make my country behave ethically."

"*You're* the one who's not behaving ethically," Tom told her, and the two immediately plunged into a debate that they'd obviously hashed and rehashed before. Miranda felt she needed to stop their argument, but she knew that when she did, she would have to say something herself.

XXI.

DNR

M att loved the visitation part of his first pastorate much more than any of his other duties, so he moved into hospital chaplaincy and found it to be a rewarding ministry location. He had earned the necessary educational qualification and obtained the appropriate certification and was employed as a chaplain at a regional medical center.

One of his seminary professors had maintained, "If you are there with people when the cup of life is overflowing with joy or sadness, they will forgive anything you might say in the pulpit." Matt felt he had a wonderful job because it allowed him to share those "overflowing" moments with so many people and relieved him from having to cope with problems of congregational leadership. He also appreciated the opportunity to work with people from all sorts of religious backgrounds and even those who had no religious affiliation at all—he actually found some of the latter to be among his favorite patients.

Part of Matt's responsibilities was to work with patients who wanted to complete Do Not Resuscitate (DNR) orders before undergoing surgery or other risky procedures. He had received training and certification for that task and was skilled at walking patients through the somewhat complicated paperwork. He was conscientious about making sure the DNR was included on a patient's chart and that the appropriate placard was posted at the foot of the bed. He felt confident that he was performing a valuable ministry when he helped patients make decisions about dying that were the right decisions for them.

Nevertheless, he found himself thinking one evening in springtime that he had never encountered a patient quite like Paula. At age thirty-six, she was faced with a diagnosis that required her to have a fairly serious operation. She had been basically healthy throughout her life, and her physician expected the surgery to eradicate her current problem completely. When Paula signed the consent form the evening before her early-morning procedure was scheduled, she was told that although she was expected to make a full and complete recovery in a relatively short period of time, there were always some risks associated with surgery done under general anesthesia. When she asked directly, "You mean I might never wake up?" she received the honest answer, "That's very unlikely, but it is possible."

She signed the form. After she had been alone and had thought about it for a while, she rang for the nurse and said that she didn't want to be brought back if she died on the operating table. When she ascertained that what Paula was talking about was a DNR order, the nurse paged Matt and asked him to visit her with the needed paperwork. "It's an unusual case," the nurse told him. "She's young, but she said she has no family members who need her, and that she's just 'ready to go if it's her time.' I hope maybe you can talk her out of it."

Matt gave a noncommittal reply, as he had experienced health care professionals who had a hard time "letting go" of a patient before. Still, he felt that it would be strange for a nurse to become over-attached to a patient so quickly. When Matt entered Paula's room, he found the patient reading a copy of *People* magazine. She put it down as he entered, and when he introduced himself, her face assumed a slightly stubborn expression. "I guess you're going to try to talk me out of this like that nurse did," she said, "but if God wants me to die now, then that's what ought to happen."

"Whether you sign the order is up to you, of course," Matt said, "but may I ask you what it is that's prompted you to make this decision? I usually talk through the process with patients, and most people find it helpful to put what they're thinking into words."

Paula didn't immediately seem sure that he genuinely wanted to hear what she had to say, but once he convinced her that he wanted to listen, she began to tell him a bit about her family. The stories she recounted were about a grandmother and an aunt who had been "coded" during stays in the intensive care unit and who were never healthy enough to care for themselves afterward. "My momma had to take care of them for years, and she said that it was because they stopped God's hand when he was trying to take them home," Paula said.

"It sounds as if your mother might have been feeling a negative impact on her own life, too," Matt said cautiously. "What does she think about the surgery you're having now?"

"She died last year in a car wreck. See, that's another thing—I don't have anybody who'd take care of me if I got like my grandma and aunt did."

"Do you have a church family? Have you ever talked about this with a pastor or a counselor?" Matt asked.

"Well, I did ask my pastor about what my momma said, and he said that our church teaches you don't have to use heroic measures to keep somebody alive. I think he meant doctors are just people when they're doing their regular jobs, but you have to be a hero to bring somebody back when they're dead. So I don't want heroes to be working on me."

"Ah, I see," said Matt, although he didn't. He opened his mouth to add more, but discovered that he had no idea what to say, and simply closed it again.

A friend of his, a lawyer who thought extremely well but not extremely quickly, had once shown Matt how he occasionally bought time by making his cell phone's ringtone go off in his pocket as though he were receiving a call. He and Matt had the same phone, and Matt had joked around a little about some circumstances where he might use the trick to remove himself from difficult moments at the hospital. However, at the time he wasn't able to imagine a situation where he would actually resort to that measure. Now, standing by Paula's bed, he found his hand in his pocket with his cell phone. "The problem with that," he thought, "is that I'd still have to come back and finish this conversation, because the papers have to be signed—or not signed—tonight."

XXII.

Paper Chase

Being a senior pastor seemed to come naturally to Larry. He had grown up working in his parents' business after school and during summer vacations, and he had seen his parents deal effectively with employees in many kinds of situations. When he went away to college and took some management courses, he discovered that his parents had been using, apparently just intuitively, several aspects of formal management theories, especially those that called for helping employees enjoy their work and expand their capabilities.

Later, when he went to seminary, he discovered some other ways of looking at how his parents had dealt with the people who worked for them: he found theological language about empowerment and treating others as one might treat the Christ. He had come to see one task of a senior pastor as helping the members of his staff to grow spiritually and to learn to answer more fully the call of God upon their lives.

Not surprisingly, Larry's staff worked well together, and their congregation was growing steadily. The time came when they were ready to add another full-time minister whose responsibilities would include leadership of the programs for children and youth. The new associate pastor, Stephanie, was relatively young herself and quite enthusiastic about her new position. In her first six months, the youth group gained several new members and became a more visible and active part of the church.

At a staff retreat held during the slow period early in January, Larry and the staff picked out several Sundays for special church-wide emphasis in the coming year. One of them was the Sunday in April nearest Earth Day. Stephanie was excited about that choice because she was convinced that every age group among the children and youth could participate in some appropriate way.

Larry had always avoided micromanagement, and it never occurred to him to ask Stephanie for a complete rundown on what she planned to do with every single age group. Thus, he learned by reading in the draft of the April newsletter that the senior high youth were going to observe Earth Day and celebrate the gift of God's good creation by washing dishes. Specifically, they were going to wash the dishes that they hoped the adults would use instead of paper plates and cups for the coffee time that preceded the 11 o'clock worship each week. They planned to continue the project through the months of April and May and then decide whether they would extend it into the summer.

"Hm," Larry thought, "that sounds like a lot of work. I hope Stephanie doesn't wind up doing the dishwashing herself, and I'll bet they don't carry on through the summer. But it's a great idea, and it's certainly in tune with the resolution we passed at our regional conference last year to ask our conference center to avoid using paper tableware. We'll just see how it goes."

Ten days later—four days after the newsletter had been mailed out—he got a call from Stan Mitchell, a parishioner in his late sixties who made one of the larger financial pledges each year and faithfully fulfilled the obligation. Stan asked to see Larry, and they set up an appointment for that afternoon. Larry found himself wondering several times in the interim what Stan wanted to see him about; he was not the sort of person Larry expected to ask for counsel or help with a problem. It crossed Larry's mind that since Stan was a former executive who had retired a year or so ago, he might be thinking about estate planning and want some advice about making a gift to the church. Larry was always mildly uncomfortable discussing money, but he steeled himself to be ready if that was the conversation Stan had in mind.

He found himself watching for Stan's arrival, and when he saw Stan's BMW enter the parking lot, he rose and went to the door to greet him. "How's retirement?" he inquired, and was surprised to hear Stan's answer that it was not necessarily all it was cracked up to be. As Larry listened, he thought he detected an undertone of boredom in Stan's description of his new life. After awhile, he asked what in particular Stan had wanted to discuss with him.

Though he thought he was prepared for whatever Stan might say, Larry was shocked to hear him speak angrily about the youth group's Earth Day project. Within a few sentences, he made it clear that he considered the project as a personal insult to him and his former occupation.

"Stan," said Larry, "I'm sorry you're upset. I need a little help, though, in understanding how you feel this relates to your career. The paper company you worked for produces cardboard containers, don't they? I had never heard that they make paper plates and cups, too!"

"We don't," Stan replied, "but that's beside the point. What the church is saying is that people who make paper are bad. She's making me feel like my whole life was a sinful waste. It wasn't! I've done lots of good things for this church that ought to be appreciated."

"She?" Larry asked, fearing he knew the answer.

"That new youth minister," Stan said. "She's stirred the young folks up about this. There are plenty of us in this town and in this church who've made our livings making paper. Who is she to condemn us?"

"Um ... I don't think that's what she had in mind at all," Larry said. "And if you didn't make paper plates and cups, I'm not sure why you're feeling that this is aimed at you personally."

"Paper is paper," Stan said firmly, "and sin is sin. You had better stop her before she runs me off and everybody else who's had to work for a living. Somebody has to pay the bills around here." Looking at his watch, he stood up and said, "I've got to go. I have to pick my wife up at the hairdresser. She wants me to go with her to pick out a lamp. She's been buying lamps without me for forty-four years, and I don't see why I have to get involved now."

"Stan, could we talk some more about this tomorrow or the next day?" Larry asked. "I see that you feel very strongly about this, but I'm not sure I understand all I need to about your objection to the project."

Stan made an appointment to return to see Larry two days hence. When he left the office, Larry just sat there, wondering, "How could I have been so wrong about why Stan was coming in? What will I say to him day after tomorrow? And I better talk to Stephanie today."

XXIII.

Thin Ice

S heila had learned in seminary that it was rare for congregations of two different ethnicities to be able to share a building successfully, but when she became a regional executive and inherited responsibility for helping a relatively new Spanish-speaking congregation in a nearby city find a larger place for worship, the financial benefits of letting the El Buen Pastor congregation rent space in a large church building occupied by the Brookside congregation, a rapidly declining Anglo group, seemed too significant to ignore. Brookside would maintain their regular Sunday school and worship times on Sunday mornings; El Buen Pastor would worship at 2 p.m. and have its youth and children's activities after the service.

Soon after El Buen Pastor's move was completed, its minister, Emilio, invited Sheila to come and preach. It would be the first opportunity for her to meet most of the congregation. They settled on a date six weeks hence, during Advent, which was the first Sunday that Sheila had no other afternoon commitments. Sheila's high school Spanish was way too rusty—and in fact, had probably never been adequate—for her to preach in Spanish, and so Emilio would translate.

As she drove the highway between her city and the church where she was to preach that Sunday afternoon, Sheila looked at the bare trees in the pale winter sunlight and noticed other signs that winter was really taking hold in their area. She had put her heavy coat in the car, but since the new vehicle that came with her new job was equipped with technology that let her start the engine and warm it up while she was still inside her house, she hadn't had to wear the coat when she left home. She was wearing a long-sleeved dress and a jacket, and the car's heater kept her warm all through the journey. When she arrived at the church, she was able to park so close to the door that she just ran in without bothering with the coat.

When she got inside, the people gathered in conversation groups in the hallway were wearing coats, and she thought they must have all arrived just before she did. She felt somewhat cold. "I must have gotten more chilled than I realized between the car and the door," she thought. It was soon time for worship, and when the group moved into the sanctuary, they walked right past the coat rack, still wearing their outer garments.

Sheila took her place behind the pulpit in a chair next to Emilio. He was wearing a robe and stole, and Sheila wished she had brought hers instead of assuming the congregation would be an informal one. If nothing else, at least it would have kept her warmer, and she felt more and more chilled as time went on. During the offertory, she asked the pastor, "Is the heater broken?"

"No," he replied, "it's not on."

"Well, can't we turn it on?" she inquired.

"No," he said. She expected him to continue with an explanation. Instead, he offered to let her wear his robe. At that point, the Doxology began, and she said, "I have time to get my coat from the car." She ran out and came back in with it just as the congregation was sitting back down. The pastor introduced her, and she stepped to the pulpit wearing her coat. She had never preached in a coat, and she found that it constricted her movements and distracted her thoughts. Even with it on, she was so cold that she could hear her voice shake from time to time, and she felt that her nose must be glowing.

She and Emilio walked to the back of the sanctuary after the benediction, and before the first parishioner approached, she asked again about the heat. Emilio looked embarrassed as he told her that Brookside had placed a lock on the room where the main switch to turn the heater on and off was located. "They do not want us here," he said. "We are looking for another place to have church."

Just then, the congregants began to emerge. Even those with children, who were supposed to have Sunday school after worship, were leaving, and Sheila could hardly blame them. It was not until everyone else had left that Sheila was able to ask Emilio for an explanation. "I had a meeting alone with them, and came back for another meeting when you were there, and they agreed they would do this. What's gone wrong?"

Emilio looked upset as he responded, "We have not done anything wrong. We have done just as we agreed. They just don't want us here."

"I didn't mean *you* did something wrong," Sheila said quickly. "I just meant, what happened?"

Emilio said he did not know why the Brookside congregation was being inhospitable. Sheila decided she was just the person to find out, and she used her cell phone to call Cecilia, Brookside's pastor. A machine picked up, so Sheila left a message for Cecilia to call immediately. Since there was little else she could do, Sheila drove home, being as thankful for a car heater as she had ever been.

Cecilia did not call that evening, and the next morning when Sheila got to the office, there was no message waiting. She called Cecilia first thing and found her in her office. When she asked why Cecilia had not called, Cecilia claimed not to have received Sheila's message. "What did you want?" she asked.

Sheila recounted her experience the previous afternoon, including Emilio's assertion that Brookside had locked up its heater switch, and asked, "Do you know anything about that?"

"Oh," replied Cecilia, "I didn't realize you were going to be there. I'm sure Blake would have . . ." and her voice trailed away.

"Blake?" Sheila prompted.

"Yes, you know Blake Winberry, I'm sure; he's not the chair, but he's a mainstay on the board of trustees."

"Did I meet him at the meeting when Brookside voted to have El Buen Pastor share the building?"

"Oh, no, you didn't," Cecilia said. "He and his wife were vacationing and then visiting their son in California this fall. Nobody thought to call and tell him about the meetings."

In a flash, it became clear to Sheila what had happened, but she wanted to be sure. "And he turns the heat off after your service is over?"

"We were just sure the building would still be warm enough at 2 o'clock," Cecilia said. "I'm so surprised it wasn't."

"And he installed a lock on the door to the room with the heater switch?" Sheila pressed on.

"Yes, he figured—we figured they would forget to turn the heat off if we left it on for them. Blake says we just can't afford to heat the building Sunday nights, too."

"You mean you leave it on the other nights?"

"Oh, yes, it's too cold when we come in every morning if we don't."

"Isn't it too cold on Monday mornings? Wasn't it cold when you came in today?"

"Well, we've started dressing extra warmly on Monday mornings," Cecilia explained. "And it's only until El Buen Pastor decides to leave."

"I take it that what you're really saying is that when Mr. Winberry got back to town, he objected to the presence of a Latino congregation in 'his' building," Sheila said.

"That's exactly it!" Cecilia said. "And we didn't want to tell them to leave because we didn't want to hurt their feelings, and we didn't want to upset you, either. If they decide themselves, it will be so much better. I'm so glad you understand!"

"I understand that you need to come to my office," Sheila said. "Now."

After she hung up, she swung her desk chair around and gazed at a round spot on the wall where the stain on the paneling was lighter than the surrounding area. Her predecessor had told her that the spot showed where he had beaten his head on the wall. "I wonder why I thought he was joking?" she said aloud. She swung back around and silently pondered what mistakes she had made that contributed to the situation and how she could possibly help resolve it; simultaneously, she discovered that the mechanism on the chair allowed her to rock back just far enough for her head to reach the wall.

True Colors

Riverview Church is in a residential area on the outskirts of a small city. Rick, the pastor, is the only full-time member of the staff, which also includes a secretary and a musician, both of whom work part time. The church, founded about forty years ago, has an average attendance of about 100 on Sunday mornings.

Having been at Riverview for a little over two years, Rick had pretty much settled into a weekly routine for accomplishing his major pastoral duties. On Thursday mornings, after two hours of study and meditation on the Scripture texts for Sunday and some rough drafting work on his sermon, he made hospital calls or other needed visits.

About midmorning on a Thursday in mid-November, he finished the first draft of his sermon and went to his secretary's office to inquire whether there might be news of hospitalizations or illnesses of which he should be aware. Rachel, a member who had worked four mornings a week at the church for nearly a dozen years, had a good knowledge of the congregation, and members were accustomed to letting her know when they needed a visit from Rick.

The congregation was not an especially large one, but the parishioners were not as young as they once were, and it was a rare occasion indeed when there was no one Rick especially needed to visit on his primary visiting day. Rachel seemed a little surprised herself when she responded to Rick's query that day by saying that there was not a single person on her list.

After standing in silence for a moment or two, Rick picked up her copy of the church directory and remarked that he might actually be able to get around to visiting some of the families who had become inactive before he arrived, a task that always seemed to get pushed aside by more pressing matters. However, just as he was noticing anew that there were plenty of inactive members he could choose from, the door opened and a man struggled in clutching a rather long box, which he had to turn sideways to fit through the door, and holding the corner of another, smaller, softer package in his teeth.

"Here, Leonard, let me help you with that," Rick said, and he took the smaller package while Leonard set the long box on the floor. "Just a minute," Leonard said, "there's one more," and he darted back out the door.

"I've never seen him here during the week before," Rachel commented while he was gone. "They say he's kind of a handy man, and some folks thought that he might do some volunteer work around here since he's retired—as you know, there's always something that needs fixing—but he just wasn't interested."

Before she could say more, Leonard staggered back in with a large rectangular box that was obviously very heavy. After putting it down—thus taking up most of the empty floor space in Rachel's office—and making an effort to regain his breath, he retrieved the smallest package from Rick and announced, "I've brought you a present! Or, at least, I've brought the church a present. Same thing."

He whipped out a pocket knife and proceeded to open the smallest of the packages, talking all the while. He explained that he and his wife had been to visit her parents in a nearby town the weekend before—that's why they hadn't been in church the past Sunday—and had attended a Veteran's Day parade while they were there. "Her folks bought a condo on the third floor of a renovated apartment building. I told them they were crazy, that the elevator won't work when the power's out and then what are they going to do? Anyway, it has a balcony, and we went out there to watch the parade. It was so inspiring to stand up there and see the band go by and the kids out front marching, holding the flag. It made Jenny and me feel so *good*. We just need to get back to our Christian roots in this country, so I went out this morning and got the Stars and Stripes for the sanctuary," he said, cutting the last of the tape on the package and pulling an American flag out for Rick and Rachel to see. "There's a flag pole in these other boxes. Come on," he urged Rick, "let's go to the sanctuary and see where this can go!"

He charged out of the room, still holding the flag, without noticing the fairly stricken look that Rick felt sure must be on his face. The pastor glanced at Rachel, and she murmured quickly, "There's a story here! Come back and hear it before you do anything."

Rick nodded, and hurried to catch up with Leonard, who was impatiently holding the door to the sanctuary open. As soon as Rick got to the door, Leonard took off, chattering about what location would give the new flag its very best visibility. Rick said as little as possible at first, letting Leonard go on about how much he despised people who didn't love America and how it was going to be up to the church to teach patriotism, "the way it used to do." When Leonard had decided where the flag should be, he laid it on the communion table and said to Rick, "Come on, let's go get the pole and put it together."

"Wait just a minute," Rick said. "To begin with, the Worship Committee would have to be involved in making a decision to change the set-up in the sanctuary. And a lot of people don't agree with putting national flags in churches, you know. We can't just put this in here on our own."

"Don't agree with it!" Leonard exploded. "Who doesn't agree? You mean *you* don't? And what's all this about a committee? You're the preacher. You can do whatever you want in this church. Everybody knows that's what preachers do."

From Rick's perspective, the conversation went downhill from that point. When Rick continued to insist he was not going to make such a decision without the Worship Committee's approval—though still not articulating plainly his own opinion about the practice of having national flags in Christian sanctuaries—Leonard demanded to know when the committee would next be convened.

"Well, they have a meeting scheduled for Sunday afternoon," Rick admitted. "I could ask the chairperson to put this on the agenda."

"You do that," Leonard said, and he left, carrying his flag and vowing that the Worship Committee was going to hear from him. Rick returned to Rachel's office, where the boxes that held the flag pole and its base remained on the floor.

"I guess he's gone," she said. "I heard the outside door slam a minute ago."

"Where are we going to put this flag pole?" Rick wondered aloud, since the boxes obviously couldn't stay where they were.

"Well, we can put it in the storage closet in the choir room with the other ones," she replied.

"Other ones?" Rick echoed weakly, sensing he was about to hear the story she'd referred to earlier. Sure enough, she went on to recount how, after 9/11, a laywoman on the Worship Committee suggested that every Sunday service ought to open with the singing of "God Bless America" instead of the introit the choir usually used. She wanted us "to express our national solidarity," Rachel said, making quotation marks in the air with her fingers.

The choir actually did begin singing the song every Sunday, and no one said anything the first week or two, but about a month after the event, long-time members began to object. The pastor refused to end the practice. "I never did figure out what he really thought. I think he was against it but didn't have the courage to say so," she said. Nasty accusations began to be traded among the membership, and several families left the congregation. In fact, she said, several of the pictures Rick had seen as he was flipping through the directory before Leonard's arrival would have been images of people who left because they thought the blatant nationalism was not Christlike behavior. But the family of the woman who introduced "God Bless America" to the service left, too, stating that they were disgusted because the church as a whole "wasn't patriotic enough," she explained.

"What finally happened?" Rick asked. "And didn't they have flags, too? We don't have any in there now."

"No," she agreed, explaining that not long after the families who felt most strongly about the issue—both for and against—had departed, there'd been a small leak in the sanctuary that required some repair and repainting. The United States and Christian flags, which had been in place in the sanctuary as long as she could remember, had been stored away in a closet, along with some other items that had to be moved. When the renovations were complete, they simply weren't ever returned to their former places, "and I've never heard anyone say a word about it since," she said.

"But weren't Leonard and Jenny here then? Do they know all this?" he inquired.

Rachel picked up the directory and pointed to the place where the couple's names and pictures would have fallen alphabetically, but didn't, and said that they weren't included because they had joined the church only four years previously, after Leonard retired and they purchased a smaller home nearby. "They might have heard the story, but I very much doubt it. It's one of the most painful things the church has ever been through, and it's not something anybody here likes to talk about, or even remember."

"Well, they're going to have to talk about it Sunday," Rick said. "Leonard says he's coming to the Worship Committee meeting."

"Then," said Rachel, "you'll have to talk about it, too, won't you? What are you going to say?"

X X V .

The House

Paul had once read that the section of the newspaper a person reads first can be an indicator of the likelihood for a heart attack. He was pleased that the healthiest approach was to read the comics first, since that's what he did. However, he had just encountered a cartoon strip that made him question the policy. A medieval interviewer in the process of screening applicants for the position of stable hand asked a woman what her occupation was. She answered, "Housewife." When he asked, "Why would you want a job in a place like this?" she responded, "You haven't seen my house."[26] It might have been funny another day, but now it depressed Paul more than wars and rumors of wars on the front page could possibly have done—not that much international news ever made it to the pages of the daily in the city of about fifty thousand where Paul was appointed to First Church.

The irony of encountering the housewife who preferred the stable after he had lain awake the night before worrying about Zelda was something he'd have to appreciate later. He abandoned the comics, pushed aside his coffee cup, and put his head in his hands. "God," he prayed for at least the hundredth time since he'd left Zelda's house the afternoon before, "what on earth should I do?"

Paul was really not surprised that the worst problem he had ever encountered in ministry had to do with Zelda. His awareness of her troublesome personality began a month into his ministry at First Church, when the adult Sunday school class that he often attended sang "Happy Birthday" when she turned thirty-five. Instead of saying thanks, Zelda snarled, "What's to celebrate about being officially 'over the hill'? It just means I'm halfway dead now. If you cared about me, you would have let me forget about it!" Paul noticed that other members of the class didn't pay much attention to her rudeness, just shrugging in an "Oh, well, that's Zelda," kind of reaction, but he was a trifle stung, since he had turned thirty-five himself just a few months before. He wondered for a moment whether he should be more upset about getting old, before he, too, shrugged off her comments and returned his attention to the lesson.

Thinking about the incident later, he supposed it was natural for Zelda to be upset about a mid-life birthday, since she had never adjusted to the fact that her husband had left her five years ago and married a younger woman. The recent addition of a baby boy to that new household had made Zelda even angrier, and she viewed the infant as a threat who would detract from the time, interest, and money their father would be able to devote to her own teen-aged daughters, Marie, fifteen, and Nancy, fourteen.

Early on in his pastorate at First Church, Zelda cautioned Paul that he was never to come to her home because "the place is a mess." Though he might have assured another parishioner that the state of the house didn't matter, he was relieved to have an excuse not to visit her. As a widower, Paul felt he had to be careful about visits with single women near his own age. In fact, a member had once jokingly suggested that he take Zelda to a clergy Christmas party, but he knew that even if he had not made an ironclad decision never to date a parishioner, he would not have dated Zelda. That was assured by her reaction when he spoke in his first visit to her Sunday school class about the car accident that had killed his twenty-six-year-old wife, pregnant with the baby girl who would have been their first child, four years before his appointment there. While other members responded with sympathy, Zelda contributed: "Well, I hope you sued the other driver!"

In the months to come, Paul learned that Zelda's reaction mirrored what she would have done in such a situation; she seemed to have more lawsuits in motion than any other individual he had ever met. She even sued one of Marie's teachers who she felt "had it in for" her daughter. She was so litigious that Paul was surprised she wasn't a lawyer, and perhaps she would have been had she finished her education. As it was, she drove a taxi, and chose to drive the night shift "so that she could be at home when the girls came home from school." This left the girls alone all night, but Zelda insisted they were fine because they were old enough to stay alone, and besides, they had dogs that protected them.

Although she did not want Paul at her home, Zelda frequently used his free moments on Sunday and before Tuesday night Bible study to talk about her problems, but having been at First Church for a year and a half, Paul knew that Zelda was never going to take any advice he offered. Her immediate response to his suggestions was to insist that they would never work, and sometimes even to imply that he was a little dense for having thought they might. In spite of the fact that her own long-deceased father had been a minister (or possibly because of it), Zelda had an abiding hatred for the hierarchy of the church, which Paul sometimes felt extended to every member of the clergy, and at first, he wondered if his ordination kept her from valuing his advice. However, he heard grumbling from other members about her constant complaining coupled with lack of action to correct anything she complained about, and he soon realized that she never took anyone else's advice either.

Then, two days ago, on Sunday morning, she had done the completely unexpected: she asked him to come by her house the next day. His initial concern about being alone with her was alleviated when she asked him to come after school so that both girls would be home. In fact, she said, it was really them that she wanted him to talk to. When he asked what about, she said that she would prefer to tell him tomorrow. But, she said, before he came, he had to understand that she wanted the conversation to be held in confidence. "I'm a preacher's kid," she reminded him, "and my dad taught me that you preachers have to promise that whatever people tell you has to be held as a confidence between you and God."

That would have been the moment, Paul thought, to try to qualify what he could or could not keep secret. At the time, though, he had assumed she was insisting the visit be confidential because she was seeking a male perspective on dating for the girls and maybe even wanted him to talk to them about avoiding premarital intimacy. He thought the visit might be a bit awkward, but he never envisioned anything worse than dealing with teenagers' embarrassment about sex and perhaps needing to refer them to a female colleague. So he promised Zelda easily that, of course, he would keep her confidence.

On Monday, as he looked for her house number, Paul hoped he had made an error when he wrote the address, because his search led him to a ramshackle frame structure decidedly out of place in the relatively well-kept neighborhood. He knew immediately why Zelda wouldn't want anyone to see this dwelling, and his first instinct was to drive away and call with an excuse for not coming. However, at that moment, Zelda appeared at the front door, pushing a big black Labrador outside. She saw him, and he soon found himself picking his way gingerly across the filthy driveway and yard. "Lots of women aren't good at outside maintenance," he told himself. "It'll be better inside."

He was wrong. As he supposed was the case with many single men, Paul was not a fastidious housekeeper, and if he hadn't paid someone to come in every couple of weeks to do what she called "deep cleaning," the parsonage would not be as pleasant to live in as it was. Still, he could not imagine ever letting a home deteriorate into this state. As he moved through the entry hall, where he stepped around piles of decaying leaves, which he felt sure harbored insects and who-knew-what-other living creatures, to the dining room, where Zelda sat him at the table, his shock and horror grew. The house was far dirtier than the poorest, shabbiest dwelling he had ever entered, even during a former inner-city posting that regularly took him into the slums. He thought this must be the kind of house that sometimes turned up in the news, when rich elderly people were found dead in unspeakably dirty surroundings, overrun by unattended pets. He was thankful that Zelda offered him no refreshments, for he could not have brought himself to eat or drink anything off of the grimy table at which he sat. From his vantage point at the dining table, he could see only a small portion of the kitchen, for which he was deeply grateful.

What he could not avoid seeing was a door that led to the backyard. The entire bottom of the door had been broken off, leaving a jagged hole. Zelda said that the dogs had scratched away the wood. Anyone could simply reach through the hole, turn the doorknob and enter the house—if the knob had been operational, that is. There was simply a hole where the knob and lock had once been, and the door was kept shut solely by means of pushing a small table up against it. It was evident that even a child could move the table—and open the door—just by pushing against it.

Zelda called Marie and Nancy and had them sit at the dining table across from Paul. To his amazement, she began to tell him what "bad children" they were. She said that she had brought Paul there so that they would be embarrassed enough to stop being lazy and clean up the house. Dumbfounded, Paul tried to think of something to say that would not hurt the girls further and would make Zelda confront her own responsibility for the chaos and filth around them. He stated that teenagers were simply too young to deal with such a situation. Once it was straightened out, he said, they might be expected to maintain it, but no one could reasonably expect teenagers to straighten out what was here. He recommended that Zelda get counseling, but she said that she had already taken the girls to counseling and it hadn't changed their behavior at all. "No," Paul said, "I mean counseling for you."

Her face clouded, and he knew she thought he had overstepped his bounds, but he didn't care. He talked about the unacceptability of leaving the girls alone at night in a house where they could not lock themselves in. He almost laughed as he suddenly realized the guard dogs she always spoke of were not the Dobermans or Rottweilers he had assumed, but the clearly good-natured black Lab she had pushed out the door as he arrived and which failed to bark at him although he was a stranger, and the ancient setter who was sprawled at Nancy's feet.

"Do you need money to have work done on the house? I can find some resources to help," he offered. But Zelda interrupted and told him that she simply chose not to do any work on the house because she had filed a lawsuit against a chemical company who had once operated a toxic landfill near the neighborhood. It had already been settled in court that her street was too far away for the company to be liable for damages, but Zelda had filed an appeal and was "waiting for money from the settlement" to do repairs.

"Why wait?" Paul asked. "I could get you some money advanced." But Zelda insisted that repairs would jeopardize her case, an assertion that made no sense to Paul. The conversation deteriorated rapidly, but Paul got the point across that he could not allow the girls to stay in the house alone with a door that wouldn't lock for even one more night. "I'll be back," he said grimly and strode out to his car, avoiding the leaf piles as he went. He returned in about an hour with a door and lock set, which he purchased from his discretionary fund (emptying it in the process), and all the tools he possessed. He had never been much of a handyman, and he knew that hanging a door presented a challenge even for skilled carpenters, but he also knew that he did not dare bring anyone to help him. Relying on the advice the clerk at the store had given him, the fact that he had once, decades ago, watched his father hang a door, his common sense, and a great deal of prayer, Paul finally managed to get the door and the lock in place. There were two keys with the lock, and he gave one to each of the girls.

Marie and Nancy were genuinely grateful, but when he said he hoped they felt safer now, Zelda said derisively that none of the windows would lock anyway, so what difference did it make? When he told the girls that the windows could be wedged shut with sticks for the meantime, Zelda lost her composure and began to yell at him.

"You're acting like I'm doing something wrong here," she shouted. "Why don't you tell them to clean this place up?"

"If the girls are such a burden, maybe they should spend more time with their father," he suggested. But she screamed, "He beat me and beat them, too! They can't go there! Do you want them to be abused again? And here you are trying to make me feel guilty. Tell them to do what they're supposed to. I'm doing the best I can! And I warn you, if you tell anybody about this house, I'll sue you. I'll know where it came from, and I'll take you to court. And I'll bring you up on charges in the church, too! You'll lose your orders, and you'll never preach again! Now, get out of my house this minute!"

He tried to protest, but with Zelda screaming and the girls beginning to cry, it was obvious to him that his best, if not only, course was to leave. He had come home and spent much of the night trying to decide what he should do. Part of the evening was devoted to a fruitless search for notes from a peer group session from his internship, when one of the students had presented a situation that had to do with suspected child abuse. Paul could remember that an intern faculty member had informed them that it was a law that all suspected abuse or neglect be reported; however, he had gone to seminary in a different region of the country, and he didn't know the laws in his own state. He vaguely remembered the discussion having touched on Roman Catholic priests enjoying the privilege (and burden) of what was called the "seal of the confessional," which kept them from having to testify in court about anything they heard from parishioners. Ministers in his denomination, he'd been told, were betwixt and between. Though they were expected "to maintain all confidences inviolate, including confessional confidences,"[27] they had no legal protection from having to break that trust on the witness stand. His memories of the session were so vague as to be of little help a decade later, though, and furthermore, he didn't know for sure if what he'd "learned" had been accurate at the time.

Searching fruitlessly for his copy of his church's *Book of Discipline*, he finally got in his car and drove to his office, where he located the volume in a bookshelf. He sat down behind his desk, scribbled "Buy *Discipline* for house" on a sticky note and posted it on his computer screen, and then began to search the index. He soon located section 341, "Unauthorized

Conduct," which included the admonition, "All clergy of The United Methodist Church are charged to maintain all confidences inviolate, including confessional confidences, except in the cases of suspected child abuse or neglect or in cases where mandatory reporting is required by civil law."[28] A footnote referred to a Judicial Council decision that had apparently been made since Paul had studied the topic.

His body sagged as he realized, with enormous relief, that the rules had been changed to account for the kind of situation he was facing. He breathed out a whispered, "Thank God," but even as he inhaled again, his eyes widened as he was struck with the memory of standing in the hallway with Zelda, promising her that of course he would keep what happened in his visit confidential. Though the denominational change of policy had emptied her threat to make him lose his orders, he knew that she could still sue him, and the fact that she probably wouldn't win would not prevent his having to hire an attorney and go through a trial in civil court, which would constitute an enormous disruption within the congregation no matter how it turned out. Even more basically, he had to decide what his personal promise to her, specifically covering that visit, meant in terms of an obligation to Zelda.

He also had pastoral obligations to Marie and Nancy, who, he had to admit, always looked clean and healthy enough, though he couldn't imagine how. If their father had been abusive—which, with hindsight, he thought he could perhaps see some evidence for—then sending them to his home might indeed be worse than leaving them where they were. He had no idea how to approach Zelda about the matter, and he was afraid to approach the girls without her there. Would it really help the girls if he reported Zelda to, well, whomever you reported such things to?

Finally—in the sense of last *and* least—there was the problem of how he would explain it to other members if Zelda and the girls stopped coming to church, and how on earth he would deal with Zelda if they didn't.

The only thing Paul knew for sure as he cradled his head in his hands that morning was that he couldn't do nothing at all.

PART THREE

NOTES ON SELECTED CASES

Note on "A Funny Way of Showing It"

I had some trust issues with men," Nicole told Sandra. Nicole's request to meet Sandra at a coffee shop rather than at her home could, with hindsight, be seen as a possible indication that she now has trust issues with clergy as well. Clergywomen are capable of committing misconduct, just as clergymen are, and it is important for Sandra not to move their meetings from Nicole's chosen public location, even if she would prefer another setting or thinks that Nicole might be more comfortable talking about certain issues in private.

Any sexual encounter between a member of the clergy and a parishioner is a violation and a misuse of the power that rests with pastors even if they do not want such power or admit that they possess it.[29] Nicole has recently been violated by a member of the clergy, and Sandra must be exquisitely careful not to impinge on Nicole's boundaries, whether Nicole is capable of defending them well or not.

She will also need to make a referral for counseling and urge Nicole to talk about her relationship with Ed with that individual. One of the reasons most pastors limit the number of counseling sessions they will have with parishioners is that once they have discussed the deep issues that counseling should open up, some people are embarrassed and do not wish to see the counselor again in social settings. If that counselor is their pastor, they may stop coming to church, thus losing their pastor and congregation. Spiritual nourishment is also crucial to Nicole's healing, and Sandra should make sure, insofar as she can, that she remains in a position to provide it. Not discussing the affair in depth may also help maintain the boundaries that Nicole needs Sandra to respect.

However, one thing that is specifically needed from Sandra in her pastoral role is a discussion of forgiveness, especially once Nicole has learned to see exactly how it is that Ed has sinned against her. She needs to understand that forgiving is not the same as pretending an offense never happened or making herself vulnerable to the individual for a repeat of the physical abuse she suffered from her husband or the violation she suffered from Ed.

Negative reactions to the ideas of sacrificial atonement that Sandra remembers having studied in seminary can often be linked to harmful past familial relationships. Though parental images for God are not always intrinsically destructive, when we attach human images or characteristics to the Deity in an uncritical way, it can lead to trouble. One thing that Sandra needs to work on with Nicole is to help her understand that the Scriptures offer many other images to use in thinking about God and God's relation to us.

Other, deeper issues regarding the sacrificial nature of traditional atonement theory have been brought to light by the work of womanist, feminist, mujerista, and Asian women theologians. The commonly received notions of the Atonement—for example, that humanity needed to be saved by the payment of a life to the devil, or that the payment in question was actually made to God instead—leave many twenty-first-century Christians, like Nicole, feeling that the nature of the God of grace has somehow surely been misrepresented.

The very nature of the human problem itself is related to this issue. Is our basic problem a failure to obey God? Or is it better interpreted as a failure to love? Or, perhaps, even a failure to understand? The book of Job gives some hints of how to use this latter interpretation. Though Job has done nothing wrong, still he suffers. His friends urge him to admit what he has done wrong and repent. He insists there is nothing that he needs to repent for, but he does not challenge the basic truth of suffering's link to sin. Finally, he demands an explanation from God, who responds merely by demonstrating Job's lack of knowledge about how things are. At the end of a divine monologue that never provides information about any misdoing on Job's part, Job repents. The reader is left to wonder, "Repents of what?" Reflection reveals that it is Job's mistaken assumptions about God, and in particular his uncritical acceptance of the idea that if one suffers, it is because one has sinned, that he now puts behind him. Now that he knows better who God is, he no longer has to inquire why he is being punished.

Seeing our predicament as involving a failure to understand rather than simply a failure to obey requires a more complex view of what actually happened on the cross. The revelation that God is not as we thought God would be represents a way of bringing us into right relationship with God that is quite different from those represented by the "payment" motifs. It is saving work, indeed, but work that requires a profound transformation of ourselves.

Sandra might also discuss with Nicole the recognition by Valerie Saiving and many subsequent scholars that the topic of sin may need to be couched differently for women. While pride might more often be the root of other sins for men, a lack of sufficient self-regard may be the more serious problem for women. An exhortation to self-denial may be an appropriate message to deliver to some individuals, but unfortunately it is most frequently taken to heart by those who are already too prone to sacrifice their selves and their identities in unhealthy ways. Nicole's past decisions to participate in destructive relationships and her suspicion of God's "abusive" nature may be far more directly connected than she realizes, and it may be impossible to address one without addressing the other.[30]

XXVII.

Note on "The Trinity at Trinity Church"

In 1982, the Faith and Order Commission of the World Council of Churches issued a landmark document entitled *Baptism, Eucharist and Ministry* (known informally as the "Lima document" or "BEM"), reporting on the progress of discussion among Protestant, Roman Catholic, and Eastern Orthodox bodies on these three important elements of the church's life. Points of ecumenical agreement and disagreement were noted, and the document was especially attentive to points at which the different traditions seemed to be moving toward convergence even though agreement had not yet been reached. The document was issued with an invitation to each church to engage in a process of study and to respond to it officially "at the highest appropriate level of authority," so that the commission's further reflections and proposals might be informed by these responses.

In its section on baptism the Lima document notes, as a matter on which the churches are in substantive agreement, that "Baptism is administered with water in the name of the Father, the Son and the Holy Spirit."[31]

In addressing this particular point, the official response of The United Methodist Church to the Lima document remarked: "Since the biblical and traditional form for baptism with water includes the phrase, 'in the name of the Father, the Son, and the Holy Spirit,' we do not urge abandoning or changing it. Nevertheless, with the heightened sensitivity to the disproportionate masculinity of liturgical language, we are compelled to sense a certain reserve about perpetuating this form of the trinitarian name of the triune God."[32]

The "reserve" mentioned in this response has been expressed not only in the writings and conferences of professional theologians but also in the liturgical life of many local congregations like Trinity Church, from a decade or so before the Lima document's publication into the present. Various alternatives to the traditional formula have been proposed and used—in sermons, hymns, prayers, and benedictions, and (perhaps less frequently, but still noticeably) in the sacrament of baptism—in United Methodist churches and in churches of other denominations.

Meanwhile, the naming of God has come to be used by various groups as one of a number of "wedge issues" to create or exacerbate divisions within denominations. A true Christian (it is said), loyal to the apostolic faith, will use the traditional formula and countenance no other; and ministers and congregations that innovate in this matter are not performing valid Christian baptisms. Their illegitimate baptismal practice, misrepresenting the name of God and thus baptizing people into some other faith than the Christian one, is of a piece with the manifold other ways in which they are abandoning genuine Christianity, honoring a false God, and leading the innocent astray. As might be expected, this line of argument evokes a counter-charge from defenders of innovation, which often enough plays into the hands of the self-styled defenders of the faith. On this issue, as on a number of others used as wedges in the current cultural and religious contentions, the genuine multiplicity of thoughtful possibilities is whittled down to two "sides," between which there can be no compromise. Efforts to find or create a middle ground are commonly portrayed as hopelessly muddled, or as wimpy efforts at avoidance—and perhaps justly so, insofar as they are efforts to mediate between two inherently irreconcilable positions. We need another way of framing the discussion. There are in fact many views, and many approaches to be considered.

The rubrics for the baptismal service in the current *United Methodist Hymnal* (published in 1989, just a few years after Lima and the ensuing United Methodist response) state that "the essential acts in baptism are the vows and the baptism with water in the name of the Father, and of the Son, and of the Holy Spirit."[33] For many, this statement, or its like, has been perceived to settle the matter, and to rule out any permissible alternatives to the use of the traditional words. That perception is cast in doubt, however, if one entertains for a moment this question: What *is* "the name of the Father, and of the Son, and of the Holy Spirit"?

Recall that the official United Methodist response to the Lima document referred to "the Father, the Son, and the Holy Spirit" as "this form of the trinitarian name of the triune God." Are there other forms? Can the triune God be rightly and faithfully known and invoked by other names? A fair number of theologians, pastors, and congregations have been exploring this issue in recent years. Ruth Duck and the late Patricia Wilson-Kastner addressed the question together in *Praising God: The Trinity in Christian Worship*,[34] which contains a baptismal liturgy with several suggested alternative formulas. Christopher Morse[35] and David Cunningham[36] are among the systematic theologians who have given creative attention to the principles involved. One of the richest and most interesting proposals is that of Kendall Soulen, in an essay considering the Tetragrammaton, the traditional trinitarian formula, and the products of disciplined improvisation as "three inflections of the triune name."[37]

As the situation at Trinity Church suggests, these issues do not originate in scholars' studies, nor do proposed solutions receive their most important testing there. The questions raised by Mark will, if all goes well, lead to further exploration both in settings of congregational study and deliberation, and in the context of worship and proclamation. In order for all to go reasonably well, however, it will be important not to allow the matter to become politicized or polarized. It has political aspects that should not be ignored, but it should not be reduced to them. As the saying goes, everything is politics, but politics isn't everything. The real promise of this incident is the opportunity it affords for a broader and deeper understanding of trinitarian faith and affirmation on the part of the congregation, and for a more confident and vibrant witness to the same faith, not least through the sacrament of baptism.

Note on "Things That Go Bump in the Night"

Yogi Berra was right: you can observe a lot just by watching.[38] But what you observe will depend a great deal on what you are prepared to notice, and on what you are prepared (or predisposed) not to notice. In both cases, the "preparation" is of various kinds. Formal education provides a fair amount of preparation on both sides of the ledger: from elementary school through graduate professional training, we are taught to attend to certain aspects of reality, and to ignore others; to ask certain kinds of questions, and not others. In less formal but still deep-going ways, our overall life experience and ongoing socialization in a particular culture (or in more than one culture) shape our perception as well as our conscious interpretation of what we perceive. Our more specific social locations—matters associated with gender, race and ethnicity, class, sexual orientation, social environment—provide experiences and forms of training that (to put it mildly) encourage or discourage our awareness of certain things. One person's safety and survival may require constant attentiveness to features of a situation that will entirely escape the notice of others in that same situation who do not share that person's vulnerability, and who may even be responsible for it. The situation itself may be maintained by this disparity in the distribution of knowledge. The line from Upton Sinclair recently recalled by Al Gore in *An Inconvenient Truth* comes to mind: "It is difficult to get a man to understand something when his salary depends upon his not understanding it."[39] The now-dated use of "man" and "his" in Sinclair's observation may be especially apt, although gender is not the only factor in the power differentials that lead us to different knowings. Knowledge is power, certainly; but so, in an odd way, is ignorance.

Much of this is relevant to our understanding of Ginny's situation. Unless such considerations are borne in mind—and one would hope Abigail would have them firmly in mind—the immediate tendency might be to correct Ginny's "misperception" and to reassure her that her experience wasn't real. This could be fairly damaging to Ginny's self-confidence as well as to her trust in Abigail and in the Christian community and message that Abigail in some way represents to her. Anything dismissive, belittling, indulgent, or patronizing in Abigail's tone or approach would likely be readily perceived by Ginny, with quite unfortunate results. One would hope that Abigail brings to this conversation some knowledge of developmental psychology—whether through study or through her own significant interaction with children—and also of the experience of bereavement, so that she might be able not only to avoid such a misstep but also to have some initial insight into what might be going on with and within this mature nine-year-old child.

But Abigail would also not respond to the situation adequately as a Christian pastor if she brought to it only that sort of knowledge and insight, important as it is. There is a deeper dimension to be explored. The incident—meaning by that the whole experience of Ginny's loss of Cecilia, in which the unsettling event in the van was an integral moment—opens up some windows onto what is real.

Christian witness is in constant tension with reductive readings of reality. It is challenged by them (for instance, "Was Jesus *really* raised from the dead?"), and it challenges them in turn, unless it meekly submits and accommodates itself to whatever passes for "the real" in this place and time (for instance, by insisting that the Resurrection is a scientifically provable "fact," or by surrendering the claim somehow). It properly challenges these limited and limiting readings of reality by seeing all things in relation to the risen Christ (see 2 Corinthians 5:16).

What would it mean to see Ginny's experience in this context? It would mean opening up rather than foreclosing the possibilities for growth in understanding and in faith that it offers. One potentially promising resource in this connection (depending on the specific tradition and *ethos* in which Abigail and her congregation are situated) might be the concept of the communion of saints.[40] In Christian understanding, the reality of the dead for the living is not merely a sort of psychological residue. It is a continuing relationship, radically transformed by the event of death but not abolished by it. Certainly Ginny needs to come to understand that Cecilia is "really dead," and she needs to be helped, with all tact and respect, to work through whatever was at the root of the frightening and unsettling aspect of her perception of Cecilia in the van's television screen; this might have been simply the phenomenon itself, or perhaps it was something unresolved in their experience together that needs attention. But beyond all this, she, along with her mother and other companions in the congregation, can also be helped toward an envisioning and affirmation of Cecilia's life now in Christ, and toward a transformed relationship with her in light of the Gospel.

XXIX.

Note on "True Colors"

W e need to get back to our Christian roots in this country, so I went out this morning and bought the Stars and Stripes for the sanctuary." This *non sequitur* of Leonard's may be at the heart of this situation. What connection does he see between Christian worship and national purpose? What is he hoping to accomplish by placing the national flag in the sanctuary?

Evidently the congregation has had some painful experience with the tension-filled relationship between Christian faith and national loyalty in the recent past. Some members resisted what they viewed as an inappropriate blending of Christian worship with devotion to country; others wanted a still closer identification of the two. How are we to read the fact that the two flags, having found their way out of the damaged sanctuary, never found their way back in? It would be unwise to conclude from this that the issue has been resolved, or even confronted. Perhaps there has been a tacit agreement on everyone's part—that is, on the part of those who did not leave—simply to avoid it.

If the issue has lingered unresolved, this will complicate the discussion the Worship Committee is about to have with Leonard and with their pastor, neither of whom shares this particular painful history. It would be one thing if the congregation, either independently or as a part of denominational polity, had a shared understanding as to the placement of flags or other national symbols in spaces dedicated to Christian worship. There is no indication that any such understanding exists at Riverview. Leonard's plan—particularly if he presents it to the committee with the same aggressive self-confidence with which he proceeded on this morning—could reawaken old hurts and animosities, or at the least force to the surface a subject that people are very reluctant to entertain. Furthermore, the issue is likely to be posed in a way that encourages the drawing up of sides and the mounting of defenses, rather than the patient exploration of a complex set of considerations. Leonard might even have the odd experience of finding himself sidelined, while veteran members of the congregation relive the conflicts of the past.

Rick has some work to do. That work is essentially of three kinds. First, he needs quickly to become informed on the subject, so as to be able to fulfill a very necessary teaching role at the meeting. It will be important for him to be able to set a context for the discussion and to introduce information on a range of relevant considerations as the meeting proceeds. Thankfully, the Internet has made it possible for him to acquire the needed expertise in a short time,[41] assuming that he has a good basic theological education to begin with.

Second, Rick needs to get in touch with the chair and perhaps several other members of the Worship Committee to alert them to the upcoming addition to their agenda and to talk with them briefly about it. This is a vital step for several reasons. These members may well have background information and insight that will be helpful; they will be forewarned and will have a chance to take some soundings in their own memories, emotions, and convictions in connection with the matter, rather than being taken by surprise; and they can formulate at least an initial idea or two about how the discussion might be most constructively approached.

Third, Rick needs to think through his own memories, emotions, and convictions in connection not only with Leonard's problematic gift, and with flags in chancels generally, but also with the broader issues of "God and country" that will almost surely come into play, if not in the meeting itself, then in the ensuing weeks. Rick may well be of more than one mind himself, or he may have had experiences of one kind or another (military service, political confrontations, a period of living in another country and culture) that have left a deep impression on him and have formed his attitudes in ways that he may or may not recognize. He needs to know himself sufficiently to prevent distracting or subverting himself, so as to serve as a responsible and reliable guide to the people entrusted to his leadership and care as they travel through this terrain, with all its danger and its possibilities.

It is very dangerous terrain indeed: very serious values are in play. It is quite likely that some of the people who opted to leave Riverview in the post-9/11 period did so in order to keep faith with commitments made; even to entertain the question of the priority of Christian and American allegiance might seem too close to disloyalty to one or both, or to friends and family members who have given their lives in service to their country. Nothing said or done should make light of these commitments. At the same time, the journey offers possibilities for a better understanding of the ways our various proper loyalties, distinct but interwoven, can sustain and enrich one another. A good deal of tact and wisdom will be required if these possibilities are to be realized.

This third aspect of the work Rick must do in this connection is an especially crucial one not only for the present case but for ministerial leadership generally. It is well known that a person in grief over a recent loss is often reliving earlier losses as well. "Grief work" that was left undone in the earlier instance, for whatever reason, can reappear on the agenda, insistent on a hearing. What may be less widely understood is the more comprehensive pattern in human behavior of which this is a part. Unresolved issues in one's personal life may crop up at the most inopportune times—in fact, they are most likely to crop up at those times, triggered by some subliminal association, just as a scent can trigger a vivid memory. These issues can then take over, surreptitiously, seriously disrupting and distorting one's engagement with the present situation and its genuine needs. This is why the question "What is going on with you?" remains an indispensable part of the minister's discipline, not only in studying cases such as this one but also in attending to the incidents and situations of real life.

Notes

1. Randy L. Maddox, *Responsible Grace: John Wesley's Practical Theology* (Nashville: Kingswood Books, 1994), pp. 15–17.

2. Ibid., p. 17.

3. This image is from Dr. Gary Peluso-Verdend, Associate Professor of Practical Theology, Phillips Theological Seminary.

4. I have summarized their insights in "Paying Attention," *Quarterly Review* 13 (Fall 1993): 39–44. Although its importance was brought home to me in the course of my experience with this group, the idea of theology as attentiveness did not, of course, originate with them. It has a fairly ancient lineage. The writings of Simone Weil and of Iris Murdoch on the concept of attention have had some influence on more recent theological uses of it; see Simone Weil, "Reflections on the Right Use of School Studies with a View to the Love of God," in *Waiting for God*, translated by Emma Craufurd (New York: Harper & Row, 1973), pp. 105–16, and Iris Murdoch, *The Sovereignty of Good* (New York: Schocken Books, 1971).

5. There is an important strand of Christian teaching on God's activity *ad extra* that affirms that the act or activity of "creation" encompasses the entire relationship of God to the world, and that reconciliation, redemption, and so forth are best understood as aspects of that one act.

6. H. Richard Niebuhr, *The Purpose of the Church and Its Ministry* (New York: Harper and Bros., 1956), p. 113. The internal quotation is of the opening lines of John Calvin's *Institutes of the Christian Religion*; the translation is not identified.

7. My language here reflects that of Jonathan Edwards and John Wesley, but the sentiment runs much more broadly and deeply in Christian tradition. For a slightly fuller sketch, see Charles M. Wood, "Methodist Doctrine: An Understanding," *Quarterly Review* 18 (1998): 167–82.

8. I am using language from different sources here to indicate that the same basic point can be made in several ways, each with its own resonances and advantages.

9. Both the adjective and the noun in the term "Wesleyan quadrilateral" have been fairly called into question. "Quadrilateral" seems to give rise to a number of misleading inferences as to the relative standing and functions of the four elements so named, and "Wesleyan" may wrongly imply that John Wesley explicitly set forth this four-factor set as the ingredients in a "Wesleyan" theological method. "Quartet" may avoid some of the dangers of "quadrilateral"—and may, of course, give rise to new dangers of its own. As for the

Wesleyan provenance of the scheme, it should be said that while Wesley made frequent appeal to each of these factors in developing a theological argument, and would sometimes refer to two or three of them together (e.g., "Scripture and reason"), no instance seems to occur in his writings in which all four are mentioned at once. Further, as an heir of the Protestant reformers he rarely had a good word to say about "tradition" as such, but would advert to "Christian antiquity" or "our church" (i.e., the heritage and practice of the Church of England) rather than to "tradition"; he made extensive use of the work of an impressive range of Christian writers from various eras and regions. In any case, it can fairly be said that Wesley made use of all four factors, in a discriminating fashion that is represented reasonably well in the current United Methodist statement on theology. It would also be well to acknowledge he was by no means the first to do so. In his utilization of these four general resources or instruments he was drawing upon ample precedent.

10. "Theological Guidelines: Sources and Criteria," *The Book of Discipline of the United Methodist Church* (Nashville: United Methodist Publishing House, 2004), p. 76. The opening phrase, "As United Methodists," may seem limiting, but it has a certain value here. Perhaps it can be read as this body's reminder to itself of its accountability to something greater than its own preconceived judgments.

11. Karl Barth, *Church Dogmatics* I/1, translated by G. W. Bromiley (Edinburgh: T & T Clark, 1975), pp. 4–5.

12. H. Richard Niebuhr, *The Meaning of Revelation* (New York: Macmillan, 1941), p. 93.

13. "Sois la Semilla," words and music by Cesareo Gabaraín, *The United Methodist Hymnal* (Nashville: The United Methodist Publishing House, 1989), #583. (My translation.)

14. The "situation ethics" of the 1960s—developed by Joseph Fletcher, the ethicist whose story this is—was, whatever its faults might have been, an effort to rethink Christian ethics with the notion of the fitting foremost in mind.

15. Luther's scheme, which he attributes to Psalm 119, may be found in *D. Martin Luthers Werke*, Kritische Gesamtausgabe (Weimar, 1883–), 50:658, 1.29–661, 1.8. An English translation of the brief essay appears as an appendix to Gerhard Ebeling, *The Study of Theology*, translated by Duane A. Priebe (Philadelphia: Fortress Press, 1978). On the common pattern of "knowing, being, and doing" in description of the aims of ministerial education, see Gordon T. Smith and Charles M. Wood, "Learning Goals and the Assessment of Learning in Theological Schools: A Preliminary Survey," *Theological Education* 39 (2003): 17–29.

16. Clodovis Boff, *Theology and Praxis: Epistemological Foundations*, translated by Robert R. Barr (Maryknoll, N.Y.: Orbis Books, 1987).

17. Isaiah Berlin, "The Hedgehog and the Fox: An Essay on Tolstoy's View of History," *The Proper Study of Mankind: An Anthology of Essays*, edited by Henry Hardy and Roger Hausheer (New York: Farrar, Straus and Giroux, 1997), p. 436. The hedgehog's "one defence," presumably, would be its ability to roll itself into a tight ball whose spiny exterior frustrates the would-be predator.

18. I have explored this distinction and its implications for theological method in *Vision and Discernment: An Orientation in Theological Study* (Atlanta: Scholars Press, 1985; reprint edition, Eugene, Ore.: Wipf & Stock Publishers, 2000), chapter 4.

19. Douglas John Hall, *The Cross in Our Context* (Minneapolis: Fortress Press, 2003), p. 45.

20. John Wisdom, "Gods," *Philosophy and Psychoanalysis* (Oxford: Basil Blackwell, 1960), pp. 159–63.

21. The philosophical movement or tendency known as "deconstruction" deals largely with this process, particularly in its wider social ramifications.

22. John Wisdom, "Paradox and Discovery," *Paradox and Discovery* (Oxford: Basil Blackwell, 1965), p. 138.

23. Richard M. Gula, S.S., *Ethics in Pastoral Ministry* (New York: Paulist Press, 1996), pp. 15–16.

24. Gilbert Ryle, "The Thinking of Thoughts," *Collected Papers*, volume 2 (London: Hutchinson & Co., 1971), pp. 480–96. The term was later made popular by the anthropologist Clifford Geertz (who cites Ryle as his source) through his influential article, "Thick Description: Toward an Interpretive Theory of Culture," *The Interpretation of Cultures: Selected Essays* (New York: Basic Books, 1973), pp. 3–30.

25. The report was initially published in pamphlet form: *The Relation of the Church to the War in the Light of the Christian Faith* (New York: Federal Council of the Churches of Christ in America, 1944). The organizing scheme is set forth on pp. 8–9, from which the passages quoted here also come. The members of the commission, as listed at the conclusion of the report, were Edwin E. Aubrey, Roland H. Bainton, John C. Bennett, Conrad J. I. Bergendoff, B. Harvie Branscomb, Frank H. Caldwell, Robert Lowry Calhoun, Angus Dun, Nels F. S. Ferré, Robert E. Fitch, Theodore M. Greene, Georgia E. Harkness, Walter M. Horton, John Knox, Umphrey Lee, John A. Mackay, Benjamin E. Mays, John T. McNeill, H. Richard Niebuhr, Reinhold Niebuhr, William Pauck, Douglas V. Steere, Ernest Fremont Tittle, Henry P. Van Dusen, Theodore O. Wedel, and Alexander C. Zabriskie. A slightly abridged version of the report is available in *War in the Twentieth Century*, edited by Richard B. Miller (Louisville, Ky.: Westminster John Knox Press, 1992), pp. 71–124. The central section, embodying the report's major doctrinal insights, is to be found in the various editions of *Creeds of the Churches*, edited by John H. Leith.

26. Brant Parker and Johnny Hart, "The Wizard of Id," *New Orleans Times-Picayune*, 31 July 2001, E–6, copyrighted by Creators Syndicate, Inc.

27. *The Book of Discipline of the United Methodist Church 2000*, paragraph 332.5 (Nashville: United Methodist Publishing House, 2000).

28. *The Book of Discipline of the United Methodist Church 2004*, paragraph 341.5 (Nashville: United Methodist Publishing House, 2004).

29. Peter Rutter's *Sex in the Forbidden Zone: When Men in Power—Therapists, Doctors, Clergy, Teachers, and Others—Betray Women's Trust* (New York: Fawcett Crest, 1989) is perhaps the best volume ever written on this topic. Though it is now out of print, it can be found in many libraries and on used book Web sites. The Reverend Dr. Marie Fortune, founder of what was formerly the Center for Prevention of Sexual and Domestic Violence, has done pioneering work in the field of clergy sexual misconduct. The international, multi-faith, Seattle-based organization that is now called FaithTrust Institute offers helpful resources for learning and teaching. Information can be obtained at http://www.faithtrustinstitute.org.

30. Valerie Saiving Goldstein, "The Human Situation : A Feminine View," *The Journal of Religion* 40 (1960): 100–12.

31. *Baptism, Eucharist and Ministry*, Faith and Order Paper #111 (Geneva: World Council of Churches, 1982), p. 6.

32. *Churches Respond to BEM: Official Responses to the "Baptism, Eucharist and Ministry" Text*, Faith and Order Paper #112, edited by Max Thurian (Geneva: World Council of Churches, 1986), pp. 184–85.

33. *The United Methodist Hymnal* (Nashville: The United Methodist Publishing House, 1989), p. 32.

34. Ruth C. Duck and Patricia Wilson-Kastner, *Praising God: The Trinity in Christian Worship* (Louisville, Ky.: Westminster John Knox Press, 1999).

35. Christopher Morse, *Not Every Spirit: A Dogmatics of Christian Disbelief* (Valley Forge, Pa.: Trinity Press International, 1994).

36. David S. Cunningham, *These Three Are One: The Practice of Trinitarian Theology* (Malden, Mass.: Blackwell Publishers, 1998).

37. R. Kendall Soulen, "'Hallowed Be Thy Name!' The Tetragrammaton and the Name of the Trinity," *Jews and Christians: People of God*, edited by Carl E. Braaten and Robert W. Jenson (Grand Rapids, Mich.: Wm. B. Eerdmans Publishing Co.), pp. 14–40.

38. As quoted in the *New York Times*, October 25, 1963: "You can observe a lot by watchin'." *The Yale Book of Quotations*, edited by Fred R. Shapiro (New Haven: Yale University Press, 2006), p. 58.

39. Upton Sinclair, as cited in *The Yale Book of Quotations*, edited by Fred R. Shapiro (New Haven: Yale University Press, 2006), p. 712.

40. For a welcome recovery and reinterpretation of this concept, see Elizabeth A. Johnson, *Friends of God and Prophets: A Feminist Theological Reading of the Communion of Saints* (New York: Continuum Books, 1998).

41. The Web sites of major denominations provide valuable resources for just such eventualities. See, for example, the worship homepage of the General Board of Discipleship of The United Methodist Church (http://www.gbod.org/worship/), which links to an article by Hoyt Hickman, "Should We Have Flags in the Church? The Christian Flag and the American Flag," at http://www.gbod.org/worship/worship/articles.asp?act=reader&item_id=2832&loc_id=9,38, as well as to a brief historical treatment by Karen Westerfield Tucker, information on the U.S. Flag Code, and other useful material.

CPSIA information can be obtained
at www.ICGtesting.com
Printed in the USA
LVOW10s1604040518
576000LV00017B/197/P

9 780687 651627